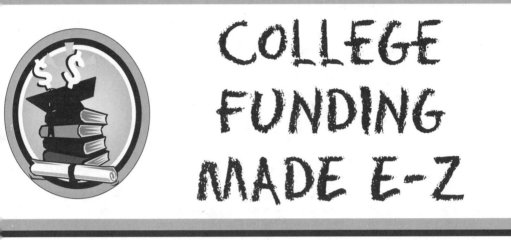

COLLEGE FUNDING MADE E-Z

Coy R. Howe

MADE E-Z PRODUCTS, Inc.
Deerfield Beach, Florida / www.MadeE-Z.com

College Funding Made E-Z™

Printed in the United States of America
MADE E-Z PRODUCTS
384 South Military Trail
Deerfield Beach, FL 33442
Tel. 954-480-8933
Fax 954-480-8906
http://www.MadeE-Z.com

2 3 4 5 6 7 8 9 10 CPC R 10 9 8 7 6 5 4 3 2

This publication is designed to provide accurate and authoritative information in regard to subject matter covered. It is sold with the understanding that neither the publisher nor author is engaged in rendering legal, accounting, or other professional services. If legal advice or other expert assistance is required, the services of a competent professional should be sought. From: *A Declaration of Principles jointly adopted by a Committee of the American Bar Association and a Committee of Publishers.*

College Funding Made E-Z™
Coy R. Howe

SPECIAL NOTE: In this product, the term "parent" refers to the collective biological parents of the student or the single custodial parent.

Limited warranty and disclaimer

This self-help product is intended to be used by the consumer for his/her own benefit. It may not be reproduced in whole or in part, resold or used for commercial purposes without written permission from the publisher. In addition to copyright violations, the unauthorized reproduction and use of this product to benefit a second party may be considered the unauthorized practice of law.

This product is designed to provide authoritative and accurate information in regard to the subject matter covered. However, the accuracy of the information is not guaranteed, as laws and regulations may change or be subject to differing interpretations. Consequently, you may be responsible for following alternative procedures, or using material or forms different from those supplied with this product. It is strongly advised that you examine the laws of your state before acting upon any of the material contained in this product.

As with any matter, common sense should determine whether you need the assistance of an attorney. We urge you to consult with an attorney, qualified estate planner, or tax professional, or to seek any other relevant expert advice whenever substantial sums of money are involved, you doubt the suitability of the product you have purchased, or if there is anything about the product that you do not understand including its adequacy to protect you. Even if you are completely satisfied with this product, we encourage you to have your attorney review it.

Neither the author, publisher, distributor nor retailer are engaged in rendering legal, accounting or other professional services. Accordingly, the publisher, author, distributor and retailer shall have neither liability nor responsibility to any party for any loss or damage caused or alleged to be caused by the use of this product.

Copyright notice

Table of contents

Chapter 1

Introduction to College Funding Made E-Z

What you'll find in this chapter:

- The importance of a college education
- When to start planning
- Beginning the process
- An overview of this guide

The entire college selection, preparation and funding process has become such a complex and difficult procedure most students and parents simply have no idea of what to do or where to start. The common questions are: What to do first? How to find the best college? How to find financial aid? What are the deadlines? What forms are mandatory? Where to find all the answers? These questions (and many more) are facing the students, and families of those students, across the United States today who are preparing for college.

The importance of a college education

We are sure that everyone reading this guide will agree with us regarding the importance of a college education. In fact, a college education is actually

> note: The United States Census Bureau says that over a lifetime, those people with college degrees will earn more than twice as much as those without a degree.

an absolute necessity for the future of any young adult. In today's society and the fast paced job market that supports it, a college education is the most vital asset any young adult can have.

The need for a college education is not really the question. How to find the best college, receive the highest quality of education, and do all of this within the student's and the family's budget is the real dilemma facing students and parents today.

There are over 3,500 institutions across the country that may be classified as colleges, universities, or specialty schools. Each and every year there are over 2.6 million students who enroll at these institutions for the first time.

The history of college preparation and funding

Before we get into the detailed workings of this guide, let us give you some history behind the college selection and preparation process, as well as the financial aid part of the scenario.

It is a fact that a college education is expensive, very expensive. Even at lower-priced, state-supported colleges a four-year degree still costs in excess of $50,000. Tuition increases at these institutions over the past few years have often doubled the rate of the cost of living increases and, consequently, made paying for a college education practically impossible.

> HOT spot: A four-year bachelor's degree at many of the private colleges and universities across the country costs $100,000 or more.

In a survey conducted by the American Council on Education, which was taken in May of 1998, it was found that financing their children's college education is one of the top five concerns facing American parents today. Although parents most generally have good intentions, there are so many unforeseen circumstances along the way that prevent them from saving a sufficient amount of money to pay for their children's college education. With today's economy, and the inflation we have experienced over the past twenty years, this problem is far more evident now than it ever has been in the past. Nowadays it often takes two incomes just to meet the family's budget. Unfortunately, after paying the family's monthly expenses, there is usually not a lot left over to set aside for the student's college education.

Students and their parents are then faced with this tremendous predicament: How does the student receive the highest quality college education and be able to pay for it at the same time? Everyone knows a college degree is a must. Everyone also knows that this college degree will be very expensive to obtain. Unfortunately, most people also know they have not been able to save an adequate amount of money to pay for this costly, but essential, education themselves. Paying for college is probably the most confusing and biggest financial obligation the student and family will ever face.

Fortunately, there are answers. There is money available to help the student and the families pay for the cost of a college education. In fact, by using the strategies and ideas outlined in this guide, the student may attend practically any institution where they are offered admission at a fraction of what they originally expected to pay.

> *note*
>
> There are, in fact, ways to achieve the student's ultimate goal, which is to receive the highest quality of education at the most affordable price.

According to the United States Department of Education there are approximately 16.7 million students enrolled in post-secondary education institutions across the country today. More than half of these students receive some form of financial aid. The federal government underwrites over 70% of all available financial aid. These available funds from the government total over $60 billion. Around 60% of these available monies are in the form of loans, while 40% are in the form of grants. The average loan of a student who graduates with a bachelor's degree is $13,500.

Although more than half of the government's financial aid is in the form of loans, an aid package containing mostly grants (money that does not have to be paid back) is a distinct possibility if the college preparation and funding maze is navigated correctly.

Financial aid is now a very vital and important part of the entire college process and is very instrumental on every college campus around the country. Even the highly priced, selective colleges and universities are offering more and more financial aid from their personal aid sources. Based solely on the reputation of the college or university, these institutions are able to attract students who are willing to pay the full cost of attendance with no discounts. This frees up additional financial aid for these institutions to offer to middle and low-income students in order to diversify their campuses. These colleges are admitting more and more students without regard to their financial need and/or their ability to pay the full sticker price of admission.

Although the goal of receiving the best possible college education at the lowest possible cost is definitely attainable, it will require hard work and dedication to achieve. Devising a plan and sticking to it through the entire college selection, preparation and funding process is a must. Students with a definite plan will always do much better than those without.

HOT spot Knowing all the sources of financial aid, the most effective way of locating, applying and obtaining that financial aid and the steps involved in the entire process are the keys to paying for college.

When to start planning

As more and more students enter college, and the financial aid system balances between supply and demand, financial aid offices will be forced to use their limited funds to attract the strongest applicants. These strongest applicants will be those students who demonstrate the most convincing record of academic and extracurricular achievement. These are the students who will most likely receive the most lucrative financial aid packages.

HOT spot
The student's accomplishments and high school achievements will mean very little if they are not portrayed to the colleges and universities in an effective, timely manner.

There are several chapters in this guide that outline how to make the student's achievements shine for the colleges in the applications for admission, application for scholarships and other financial aid, and during the campus visits.

Most college's financial aid officers now know, and agree, that financial aid will simply not be disbursed to students who ask for it. It will be awarded to the students who effectively portray their high school achievements to the colleges and universities.

Ideally students should start the college preparation process early in high school—in their freshman or sophomore year. We realize that everyone who reads this guide is not, unfortunately, a high school freshman or sophomore. Although this guide is designed to start early in the student's high school years, it is still very possible for juniors and seniors to successfully navigate the college preparation and funding maze. This does, however, require extra effort and dedication. With hard work on the part of the student and the parents, and by

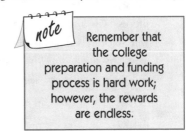

note
Remember that the college preparation and funding process is hard work; however, the rewards are endless.

arranging a personal plan of action from the information contained in the timeline and procedures outlined in this guide, this becomes a very attainable goal.

Beginning the process

When students begin looking for colleges and universities they think may be right for them—an institution where the student will excel as a person and as a student is the ultimate goal—they should keep one very important thing in mind. Do not rule out any college or university simply because you cannot afford the cost of attending. By far, the most common mistake that so many students make is going to a college down the street, or a college that brother or sister or mom or dad went to, a college they chose only because they thought it was all they could afford. This is not the correct way to select a college.

With the proper plan, you may end up paying a fraction of the cost of attendance and be able to attend a much better institution and consequently receive a much higher quality of education.

Overview of this guide

This guide is divided into three basic, easy-to-understand sections. The first section is our *Timeline*, which is the heart of this guide. The *Timeline* is a comprehensive 4-year calendar containing all the steps necessary to successfully complete the college selection, application, and financial aid process. The *Timeline* will provide you with the perfect plan to ensure you will not miss a single form, or a costly deadline along the way. This unique month-by-month *Timeline*, which is found in Chapter 2, outlines for students and their families the sequential process to follow in order to successfully navigate the college preparation and funding maze.

Students should pick up the timeline from where he/she is currently in his/her high school career. The student should make every effort necessary to catch up on any previously missed steps, while, at the same time, following all the procedures necessary for the upcoming steps.

For example: if the student is starting the junior year, he/she should start the *Timeline* at that point and go back over the previous year to make up all the steps possibly missed.

If the student does not start the procedures outlined in the *Timeline* during the high school freshman or sophomore year, he/she should still be able to achieve the ultimate education goal. However, catching up on the past requirements, in addition to completing the present tasks, will require a little extra effort; but the benefits will surely be seen.

The *Timeline* contained in Chapter 2 gives the student and parents a track to run on. It eliminates all indecision, headaches, and worry. It gives them piece of mind to know they will meet all of the necessary, important, and costly deadlines and submit all required forms in a timely and effective manner. Even though you may not be reading this guide as a high school freshman or sophomore, with the steps outlined in the *Timeline*, and a little extra effort on your part, you will still be able to successfully navigate the college preparation and funding maze.

Next, the student and family will be referred from the *Timeline* to specific chapters, Chapters 3 through 17, in the guide. These chapters contain detailed information and step-by-step instructions on how to effectively and completely accomplish each and every specific step along the way.

The third section of this guide, Chapters 18 through 23. is devoted to the following: mistakes to avoid, facts and ideas to help the student receive the maximum amount of financial aid, phrases, terms, and definitions. Also contained in these chapters are complete lists of phone numbers and addresses to assist in locating all of the various sources of financial aid, as well as tracking the progress of all the student's applications. In addition, there are several web-site referrals for easy access to helpful Internet sites.

All of these reference sources and the chapters that cover the hints, tips, and ideas should be used in conjunction with the step-by-step procedures outlined in Chapters 3 through 17.

By tying all of this information into the *Timeline* (Chapter 2), the student and family will definitely have a plan of action to successfully navigate the college preparation and funding maze.

Chapter 2

Timeline

What you'll find in this chapter:

- The timeline process
- Unique four-year plan
- Month-by-month steps and procedures
- Diary of deadlines

The following *Timeline* is designed to help both students and parents with the complicated, and often confusing, task of navigating the college preparation and funding maze. The *Timeline* begins in the student's high school sophomore year and runs through his or her freshman year of college.

We realize that everyone who is reading this is not a sophomore in high school, and will not be able to start the process from the beginning. For those of you who are past the sophomore year, we would suggest that you take the point in the *Timeline* that coincides with your present status (grade level) and begin from there. In addition, it will also be necessary for you to look back on the *Timeline* and make up any previous items you may have missed.

Remember that the college preparation, selection, and funding process is a highly sequential procedure. Each and every step along the way works together and must be completed as such. Making up any past tasks which you have missed is essential for achieving your goal, which is receiving the highest quality of education at the most affordable price.

The *Timeline* is designed to give you a month-by-month agenda to follow. In addition, it refers to the pertinent chapter(s) in the guide that will help you successfully complete each and every step along the way. You may always refer back to the *Timeline* and then turn to the chapter(s) that apply to your particular task.

High school sophomore year

First semester

1) ____Student should be an active participant in two or three selected organizations and/or clubs. This experience will be beneficial to the student's future. These will also serve as great assets later in the student's educational career when it comes time to apply for financial aid, scholarships, and admission to college.

2) ____Student should begin to explore career options.

Second semester

1) ____Student should begin a scholarship file. Included in this file should be a list of private scholarship sources. Covered in Chapter 8.

2) ____Student should continue involvement in clubs and organizations.

3) ____Student should begin considering teachers for recommendation letters to be included in college admission applications. Covered in Chapter 7.

4) ____Student should take PSAT for the first time. Covered in Chapter 5.

5) ____Student should plan their schedule for junior year.

6) ____Student should begin a list of important factors (location, size, enrollment, etc.) to consider when creating a list of possible colleges.

7) ____Student may begin compiling a preliminary list of possible colleges (20-30 or more—money is not considered at this point in the process) they would like to attend. Information regarding the college's specifics (enrollment, location, etc.) may be obtained in a college guide (available in most book stores), or by visiting the college's web-site, which is accessible through the college search information contained in Chapter 6.

8) _____Student should read and review all unsolicited mail received from colleges and place interesting information into a "possibles" list of colleges file.

9) ____Student and parents should attend a college fair, and begin gathering available information about interesting colleges. A file should be created for each college or university.

High school junior year

Beginning of school year

1) ____Student should register to take the SAT, ACT, and the National Merit Scholarship Qualifying Test. Covered in Chapter 5.

2) ____Student and parents should begin investigating any institution that makes educational loans, such as banks and credit unions—and create a file on each.

3) ____Student should apply and/or register for advanced placement courses, which will allow them to take college courses while still attending high school. These courses will also prove very valuable in the college application and acceptance process. Covered in Chapter 4.

October

1) ____After reviewing results from the first PSAT, the student should take the PSAT for the second time. Covered in Chapter 5.

November

1) ____Student should attend any financial aid workshops available.

2) ____Student and parents should attend another college fair and continue gathering any information available regarding colleges the student may have an interest in. This additional information should be placed in its appropriate file for future reference.

December

1) ____Student and parents should make sure all assets are properly positioned. Selling of investments, the structuring of savings accounts, and the positioning of funds must be done by the end of December in order to maximize the student's eligibility for financial aid. This process, along with an explanation of the details, is covered in Chapter 11.

2) ____Student and family should receive and review the results from the second PSAT.

3) ____Student should begin narrowing the original college list from 20-30 down to between 6 - 10 semifinalists. Covered in Chapter 6.

January

1) ____Student should continue research into scholarship sponsors. Covered in Chapter 8.

2) ____Student should begin writing to prospective colleges to request information regarding admission and available financial aid—including

scholarship possibilities. This information should be included in a separate file for each college or university. Information from the previously attended college fairs, and interviews with high school guidance officers and/or visits to the career center, as well as information obtained through the college's web-site, should also be included in these files.

February

1) ____Student should register for the SAT II, which is to be taken in May or June.

2) ____Student should take the SAT and/or the ACT. It is preferred that the student take both tests. Covered in Chapter 5.

March

1) ____Student should continue to gather additional information regarding colleges and universities from their high school guidance office and web-sites, and include any additional information in the college's file. This process is covered in Chapter 6.

April

1) ____Student should begin running free scholarship searches from the web-sites listed in Chapter 8.

2) ____Student should follow up on career interests with additional research and personal interviews with people in the field. Covered in Chapter 3.

May

1) ____Student should contact the state's scholarship administration and inquire about available state financial aid. Covered in Chapters 8 and 10.

2) ____Student should request all private scholarship applications from the previously compiled list of sponsors. Covered in Chapter 9.

High school senior year

August

1) ____Student should continue to prepare the high school transcript, making sure all required courses are included. Student should also enroll in all courses that are important to colleges, such as the five 'solid' subjects, as well as any advanced placement courses. Covered in detail in Chapter 4.

2) ____Student should continue searching for available scholarships. Covered in Chapter 8.

3) ____Student should decide from previous research and personal interviews upon either a college major or general area of study. Covered in detail in Chapter 3.

4) ____Student and family should complete the college search and compile a list of possible colleges based on the student's interests, wants, educational needs, and accomplishments. This list should include six finalists. Remember—Don't base your college selections on money or available financial aid at this point. Base your decision strictly on your educational goals and needs—not your ability to pay. Financial aid will be covered in detail later in the *Timeline* and also in the guide. The college search process is covered in detail in Chapter 6.

September

1) ____Student should apply and prepare to take the ACT and SAT Tests for the second time. (Taking these tests more than once is advised. The highest score is generally the one that the college's admissions officer looks at.) Covered in detail in Chapter 5.

2) ____Student and family should begin planning the college campus visits. Although these visits will be conducted from November through March, planning ahead makes these visits easier and much more profitable. Covered in detail in Chapter 12.

3) ____Student should compile and arrange the information necessary for the scholarships and college's admissions applications. This 'core' information may be used universally for applications to all scholarship sponsors as well as all colleges and universities. The student will fill out the specific application form, tailor it to each sponsor or college, and include a separate cover letter for each. The core application information should contain all of the following: (Covered in greater detail in Chapters 7 and 9).

____unofficial high school transcript

____recommendation letters from:

____teachers, high school counselor

____community leaders

____business and professional people

____members of the clergy

____list of work experience

___500-word essay about an experience that has special meaning to the student. (Some colleges or scholarship sponsors may give the student a specific topic to write about in place of this type of essay.)

____A list of references who can comment on your skills and work experience

____A list of volunteer or community activities in which you have participated

____A list of positions held in school that shows leadership and responsibility

____Copies of documents and newspaper clippings verifying your awards, honors, and commendations

4) ____Student should run another on-line scholarship search from one of the free sources listed in Chapter 8.

5) ____Student may then request applications and qualification rules from each of the scholarship sponsors listed. The student does this by writing each address listed on the scholarship search report and mailing these requests directly to each sponsor by first class mail. Covered in detail in Chapter 9.

6) ____Student should immediately apply (using previously compiled core application information) to each scholarship sponsor after receiving the application and list of rules from the sponsor. Again, covered in detail in Chapter 9.

7) ____Student may continue scholarship search by contacting the possible local sponsors from the sources listed below: (Covered in greater detail in Chapter 8).

- Clubs
- Parent-teacher associations
- Veterans groups
- Professional organizations
- Corporations
- Parent's employer and unions
- Religious affiliations

8) ____Student may then follow the same procedure to apply for local scholarships as they used in steps 5 and 6 above.

Keep a checklist of all applications for scholarships so that you may monitor the progress of these applications.

Remember scholarship sponsors may disqualify you for any reason and they have no obligation to inform you of the disqualification. (Refer to Chapter 9 of this guide for more information regarding the steps involved in receiving scholarships.)

October

1) ____Student should apply for admission to 6 different colleges using the core application information that has been previously compiled. (Be sure to obtain a copy of your high school transcript, as well as letters of recommendation and your essay to include in your applications. Having your high school English teacher review your essay before submitting it is usually a good idea.) Covered in detail in Chapter 7. Be sure to keep a list of the colleges where you apply. This information will be used when completing and submitting your Free Application for Federal Student Aid, or FAFSA, which is covered in detail in Chapter 11.

2) ____You must complete and submit a CSS/PROFILE application to the CSS processing center, if required by any of your college selections. Covered in detail in Chapter 11.

3) ____Student should continue the scholarship search and application process. Covered in Chapters 8 and 9.

November

1) ____Research the colleges where you have applied, using reference guides listed in Chapter 7 to get an idea of what kind of financial aid package you may expect from each individual college.

2) ____Student and parents should attend a college financial aid workshop.

3) ____Student and family should complete and submit any additional institutional aid applications, or miscellaneous forms, required by the college(s).

4) ____Student and parents should begin the previously planned college campus visits. Covered in Chapter 12.

December

1) ____Student and family should research and familiarize themselves with all sources of financial aid. This is covered in detail in Chapter 10.

2) ____Student and parents should gather items, data, and information needed to file the FAFSA. These items are covered in detail in Chapter 11.

3) ____Student and parents should review and study Chapter 11 for procedures and strategies that may be used to file the FAFSA more effectively.

4) ____Student and parents should run a trial FAFSA application by using the web-site listed in Chapter 11. This will give you a general idea of your expected financial aid package.

5) ____Student and parents should make final preparations for filing of your financial aid forms. Covered in detail in Chapter 11.

January

1) ____Student and family should file the FAFSA (Free Application for Federal Student Aid) application with the government. This may be done on-line or by first-class mail. Covered in detail in Chapter 11. File on January 2nd, or as soon thereafter as possible—financial aid is always on a first-come, first-served basis.

2) ____Student and family should continue the college campus visits. These visits not only set the foundation for your financial aid package, they also give the student a feel for the college. Covered in detail in Chapter 12.

February

1) ____The student and the family will receive and should review a confirmation report from the CSS/PROFILE application (if a PROFILE was required by any college). Covered in detail in Chapter 11.

2) ____Student and family must submit a copy of their completed Federal tax return forms and W-2 forms for the application year to each of the final six college choices. Covered in detail in Chapter 11.

3) ____Student and family will receive the Student Aid Report (SAR) from the government. This SAR will have your Expected Family Contribution (EFC) listed on it. Please review the results and compare with your figures, and statistics—making sure you have received the proper aid package. Covered in Chapter 11.

4) ____You may correct the SAR (if applicable), using the completed, current year's tax return information, and re-submit it to the processing center. Covered in detail in Chapter 11.

5) ____Student and family should send a copy of the SAR to each of the final six college choices (unless it was necessary to correct and re-submit the SAR, and then they should wait and send the corrected copy, immediately upon receipt, to each of the college's financial aid offices.) Covered in detail in Chapter 11.

March

1) ____Student will receive and should review the corrected SAR. The student and parents should then forward a copy onto each of the final six college choices. (Mail the corrected SAR directly to the college's financial aid office.) Covered in Chapter 11.

2) ____Student should ask for an extension or pay any necessary housing deposits. Covered in detail in Chapter 13.

3) ____Student and family should finish all campus visits. Covered in detail in Chapter 12.

April

1) ____Student will receive and should accept all admission offers. The student should send a letter of acceptance to each college promptly after receiving the offer. Covered in detail in Chapter 13.

2) ____Student will receive and should accept all financial aid awards and packages. The student should return all award letters with acceptance promptly. Although you accept all award offers, you are still negotiating and deciding on your final college choice. Covered in detail in Chapters 13, 14, 15 and 16.

3) ____The student and family should do a side-by-side comparison of each college award letter and make sure the figures agree with the research they did in November of last year. If the student is not offered what is expected, or something has drastically changed in the student's, and/or parent's, life since originally applying for financial aid, a negotiation strategy for additional financial aid should be prepared. Covered in detail in Chapters 14 and 15.

4) ____Student should now make final college choice. Covered in detail in Chapter 16. Consider all of the following aspects when making your decision:

____Personal notes from your campus visits

____College location, size, and appeal

____Your personal preference

____The most appealing and complete financial aid package

5) ____Student should then double-check to make sure all financial aid award offers are accepted and submitted to the final choice college. Covered in detail in Chapter 16.

6) ____Student should then make sure that a copy of the Student Aid Report (SAR), along with a copy of the student's and family's federal tax returns, including W-2 forms, is forwarded by certified mail to the financial aid office of the final choice college. Covered in detail in Chapter 16.

7) ____Student should make sure all necessary deposits are made for on-campus housing at their final choice college (if applicable). Covered in detail in Chapter 16.

8) ____Student should continue to track the progress of scholarship applications. Covered in detail in Chapter 9.

May

1) ____Student should obtain and complete the family's section of the Stafford, Perkins, or FPLUS loan forms and submit these by certified mail to the final choice college (if applicable). Covered in detail in Chapter 16.

2) ____Student may receive and should accept all outside scholarship offers. Immediately respond to the scholarship sponsor with a letter of acceptance and also call the sponsor and personally thank the person whose name appears on the scholarship offer for the award. Covered in detail in Chapters 9 and 13.

2) ____Student should notify each college they will not attend that they are relinquishing their earlier financial aid acceptance. Covered in detail in Chapter 16.

3) ____Student should obtain and forward to the final choice college an official final grade transcript from high school. Covered in detail in Chapter 16.

4) ____Student should complete all necessary paperwork for on-campus housing at your final college choice (if applicable). Covered in detail in Chapter 16.

June – August

1) ____Student should begin a scholarship search for the next academic year. (New scholarship sponsors are available each year.) Covered in detail in Chapter 8.

2) ____Student should make sure all scholarship awards are received. If not, contact the sponsors to inquire as to the status of the award. Covered in Chapter 9.

College freshman year

September

1) ____Student should set an appointment with the college's financial aid officer to discuss the arrangements for the work-study job included in his or her financial aid package (if applicable). Covered in Chapter 17.

October – December

1) ____Student should continue the scholarship search and application process for the following school year (college sophomore year). Covered in Chapters 8, 9 and 17.

January

1) ____Student and parents should complete and submit the new FAFSA for the sophomore year financial aid package. Covered in Chapters 11 and 17.

2) ____Student and parents should complete and submit the CSS/PROFILE application for the college sophomore year (if applicable). Covered in Chapters 11 and 17.

February - March

1) ____Student and family should receive and review the Student Aid Report (SAR) from the government and resubmit with any corrections, if necessary. Covered in Chapters 11 and 17.

2) ____Student should forward a copy of the SAR to the college's financial aid office, or wait for the corrected copy to arrive (if applicable) and then forward it. Covered in Chapter 17.

May

1) ____Student will receive the college's financial aid award renewal letter and should accept it by immediately signing and returning it to the school's financial aid office. Covered in Chapter 17.

Chapter 3

Choosing your college major

What you'll find in this chapter:

- The importance of a career choice
- Choosing your course of study
- Finding your likes and dislikes
- Planning your career

> **HOT spot** Choosing a career is one of the most important decisions a student will ever make.

The student's career choice obviously sets the foundation for an entire future. In addition, this career choice will have a great bearing on the student's selection of college, the preparation, and funding procedures. Both the student and the family will be investing a great deal of time and money into the student's chosen career. This decision is an important one and should be made with careful consideration, research, and planning.

It is true that this decision will take time, effort, and research in order to make, but the payoffs will be countless, both today and for many years to come. Remember that the student is not only preparing for his/her college education, but also preparing for and investing in a future.

> **E-Z TIP** Prior to beginning a search for the best college, it is vital that the student determines a major or general area of study.

We realize those students (and their families) who are reading this guidebook are generally between the ages of 15 and 17. We further realize that at that age there are some students who may have a firm idea of what their future educational and career goals are, and, frankly, there are a great number of students who simply have not made their decision.

This chapter is designed to give the students who are still making their career decisions suggestions and ideas which may help them along the way. Or, at a minimum, help them arrive at a general area of study they wish to pursue when entering college.

HOT spot The student's college major and/or career decision, made while the student is in high school, does not need to be a final one. In fact, the average college student changes his/her mind (and major) twice.

Before beginning the college search and selection process, at least narrowing down choices to a general area of study such as business, medicine, finance, etc. is extremely important. This chapter is designed to give the student help in determining a general area of study, a major, and eventually a career. It is important to remember that this decision, like all of the other decisions in the college preparation and funding process, is ultimately that of the student. This chapter is simply designed to give the student ideas and possibly some direction in making choices.

Reasons for deciding on a major and/or general area of study

There are several very important reasons why the student should determine his or her college major or general area of study prior to the college search and selection process, which is covered in Chapter 6.

note

The three top requirements for obtaining a college degree are generally effort, time, and money.

Everyone is aware of the fact that a college degree takes years to acquire, and contains dozens of important steps along the way. When planning for your college education and degree, it becomes very vital to make the best possible decisions along the way. These decisions include (but are not limited to): courses you take and activities you participate in while attending high school, the college you choose to attend, and securing financial aid to help pay for the cost of your education.

Most decisions you will be faced with while preparing for and attending college will be directly influenced by your career choice. Keep in mind it is not vital to choose a college major while you are still in high school. It is vital, however, to determine your general career interests and arrive at an overall area of study. This will allow you to pick a college or university that offers a program which is strong in the field you have chosen.

Remember that not all students who are preparing for college have a specific college major in mind while they are still in high school. However, at least arriving at a general area of study is vital, as we will show you in the following example.

If you know that you would like to major in business, for instance, but you are not sure whether it will be in accounting or marketing, you should still search for a college that offers a strong business program. You definitely do not want to select a college that is not strong in the area of study you have chosen.

E-Z TIP

By choosing a college major, or at least a general area of study, you will also have a better idea of your debt management capabilities, based on the future earning potential of your chosen profession.

Due to the time and effort it takes to obtain a college degree, not to mention the money it costs, it is vital to arrive at a general area of study prior to beginning college. This will prevent you from wasting valuable time and money with courses that will have little or no bearing on your eventual major.

Any debt that you may incur while attending college (most generally in the form of student loans) will either be considered manageable or unmanageable based on your future employment and earning potential.

Begin to plan your career

There are several ways high school students may begin planning his/her career. We have outlined a few approaches that may work for you:

- The student should take a long, close look at likes and dislikes, the things that interest him/her and things that don't, hobbies, travel, what lifestyle has appeal, and whether he/she enjoys working with people. These are all questions that will give the student ideas regarding a future career.

- The student may also wish to consult with a high school guidance counselor. Most guidance offices (or career planning offices) have publications listing a variety of different career options and employment ideas for various career fields. Many high schools also offer personality tests, which will help students further determine their job suitability. Also, the guidance counselor may be able to offer a professional opinion based on personal knowledge of the student.

- Meeting with people who are in the field the student is considering is an excellent way to gather additional knowledge regarding the profession. The student should make an appointment to meet with these individuals, and be prepared to discuss the advantages and disadvantages of the chosen profession. This will give the student a realistic idea of a future in that particular field.

- The student should attend career fairs, which are sponsored by high schools. These fairs offer the most recent information regarding a variety of careers.

- By participating in on-the-job training the student will get a first-hand look at the workings of a selected profession and be able to determine for himself or herself if it is something he/she would like to pursue. If the student is unable to obtain employment in the field, perhaps he/she should consider volunteering their services. Many companies offer internship positions for high school students looking for a profession to enter. These internships may be located through the student's high school guidance department, newspaper ads, or employment services.

The Bureau of Labor Statistics has many periodicals available on the subject of employment and earnings. Obtaining and reviewing this information may also give the student some direction in choosing his or her major and eventually, profession.

Chapter 4

Preparing your high school transcript

What you'll find in this chapter:

- Finding the right college
- What colleges look for in applications
- Compiling an impressive transcript
- The components of a transcript
- The importance of extracurricular activities

All colleges want good students. Most colleges look at themselves as communities, and take great pride in its residents. All colleges want students who are well rounded, with different interests, goals, and ideas. They want students who will participate and be an active part of his/her college community.

The college selection process, however, is a two-way street, and it should be approached with that in mind. While colleges are looking for students who best fit their community, students are searching for the college where they feel comfortable and are confident they will be able to excel.

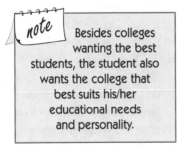

> **note** Besides colleges wanting the best students, the student also wants the college that best suits his/her educational needs and personality.

The ideal situation would be for the right student and the right college to meet. This is by far the best scenario for everyone involved. The student feels comfortable with the college, and the college is proud to have the student on its campus. This "match" makes everything else in the college preparation and funding process go much smoother. In fact, the proper match can make a world of difference in the quality of education the student receives, as well as in the amount of money the education ends up costing the student and the family.

Although finding the right, or even perfect, match is a very complicated and time-consuming process, it is a process that really should be completed, as it can be worth thousands of dollars and greatly affect the quality of the student's education, degree, and future.

This entire process starts early in your high school years. In fact, the earlier you are able to start preparing, the better. You must remember that there are several steps involved in the college selection process and they start with preparing yourself while in high school, which is discussed in detail in this chapter. The other two steps involved in this process are the college search process, which is covered in Chapter 6, and the college admissions applications, which is covered in Chapter 7. You will learn in these chapters that during your college selection process there will be three main thoughts to keep in mind while searching for a college:

1) The college is trying to make a favorable impression on you.

2) You are trying to make a favorable impression on the college.

3) College is a buyer's market, and you (the student) are the buyer. This is covered in detail in Chapter 12, *College Campus Visits*.

This chapter shows you how to prepare your high school transcript in order to make that favorable impression by showing you what the colleges look for in students and what they do not. We will outline for you what you should accomplish and participate in while attending high school, and we will

> **note** The courses and activities you pursue while in high school form the foundation of your future, and not only benefit you when applying to and paying for college, but also during adulthood.

also show you what you should avoid. Chapters 6, 7, and 12 will help you further in the determination of which college is right for you; but first, you must prepare yourself while you are still in high school. This is one of the most vital steps in the entire college preparation and funding process.

When you apply to the colleges, your applications will look like a full color portrait of four years of your life, your high school years. If your application includes what the college is looking for, you will have taken the necessary steps on your part in finding the perfect match.

College admission officers describe the students who are attractive to the college by using the term *special*. These *special students* are ones that the college would like to have on its campus. There are dozens of categories that may make a student attractive to the college. We will show you, in this chapter, how to look the most attractive to the colleges and possibly become one of these *special* students.

Items that are important to colleges

There are several items a college looks for when reviewing admission applications. We have provided a list of these items (in order of importance) below for you. This list may serve as a reference guide and also an outline for this chapter. This chapter goes into detail concerning each of the following subjects:

1) List of your high school courses, and the grades you received in each. We will show you what classes are expected and/or required by most colleges in order to gain admission, and how the colleges look at your final grades in each one of these classes.

2) Student's grade point average. We will discuss the importance, or relative unimportance, of the student's GPA.

3) Strength of your high school. We will cover what the college knows about your high school and how it may affect you.

4) PSAT, SAT, and ACT testing. We will discuss the pros and cons regarding these college pre-admission tests. PSAT, SAT, and ACT testing are also covered in Chapter 5.

5) Activities. We will review the activities the student may, or will, participate in, as well as the importance of each to the college.

Courses taken, grades received, and importance of each

Your high school transcript is the first part of your college admission application that is reviewed by the college's admissions officer.

> *note* Your transcript is the most important piece of information the admissions officer reviews in determining your acceptance.

The college admissions officers will first look at what classes you have taken in high school, and then look to see what grades you received in each. It is very important to the colleges to see first what you have done, and then evaluate how well you have done it.

DEFINITION

The college-preparatory curriculum is made up of five courses, often-called *solid subjects*, and are all extremely important to the colleges. Those courses are:

1) English

2) Math

3) Science

4) Social Studies

5) Foreign Language

Most colleges would like to see the student take four years of the first four courses listed above, and at least two years of a foreign language.

Most high schools offer some type of honors courses. These courses are commonly called Advanced Placement Courses and some may even be used for college credit. It is important that you investigate, as early in your high school years as possible, to determine which advanced placement courses are offered by your high school and may be available to you.

> **HOT spot** Your transcript is more impressive to admissions officers if you have taken tougher courses, or advanced placement courses, and received a few B's, than if you have taken easier courses and received all A's.

One very common question from high school students is whether an 'A' in an easier course is better than a 'B' in a little tougher course, or advanced placement course. Colleges like to see if you have challenged yourself or taken the easy road. By challenging yourself academically, the college admissions officers see that you have prepared yourself for the college work that lies ahead of you.

Before enrolling in the advanced placement courses, you must first determine if these courses are right for you. The best rule of thumb is to ask your teacher and/or guidance counselor if he or she thinks you would do well in an advanced placement course. In addition, if the grade you receive in an advanced course would probably be one step down (from an "A" to a "B"), it would benefit you to take the advanced course. If the step down could possibly be two grades (from an "A" to a "C"), advanced placement courses are probably not for you.

If your high school offers advanced placement courses and you choose not to enroll in any of them, but are more than academically capable, the college admissions officer reviewing your application will have questions as to whether or not you have adequately challenged yourself in high school. The possibility of your acceptance, regardless of your other achievements, will be greatly reduced.

HOT spot Remember, an advanced placement course will take more effort on your part; however, colleges look much more favorably at students who have challenged themselves by taking the advanced classes.

Your grade point average or GPA, and your class rank

note

Next in the line of things looked at by the college's admission officer is your Grade Point Average, or GPA, and your class rank. After reading the previous section on expected curriculum and advanced placement classes, you can quickly see that your grade point average does not have nearly the bearing on your college acceptance determination as the type of high school classes that you have taken.

The admissions officer will surely look at your grades to determine how well you have done in the classes you have taken; however, he or she will only glance at your grade point average if it is highly accessible on your transcript. The reason for this is that your grade point average can have so many variables involved that it is sometimes misleading, and therefore, not as important to the admissions officer. The colleges usually have their own formula used for figuring your grade point average by taking a mixture of the difficulty of the classes you have taken and the grades you received in each.

The colleges simply don't look that closely at your high school grade point average because they will determine your GPA themselves, using their own formula. This will ensure that all of their applicants have a level playing field when it comes to determining who is offered admission.

note

Class rank is directly affected by the courses you took in high school and your success in each.

Your class rank is looked at differently depending on the college or university. Some colleges give your class rank great consideration, while others completely ignore it in the determination of your acceptance. Easier courses, with higher grades, would push you up the class rank scale; however, that may not show the college that you have challenged yourself, and be detrimental to your acceptance.

HOT spot

A good rule to follow is to take the toughest high school courses available. Your willingness to challenge yourself will far outweigh your grade point average and/or your class rank in the eyes of the college's admissions officer.

Since class rank is determined by your grade point average, and your grade point average is not overly important to the majority of colleges in the country, your class rank is also not considered to be that consequential to most colleges.

Strength of your high school

A common myth floating around today is that colleges have an unpublished, and highly secretive, list of the high schools across the country and a rating for each. This is simply not true; no list like this exists. The colleges are, however, usually familiar with your particular high school and what it has to offer, and what its strengths are in comparison to other high schools in the region.

The college's admissions officer may also have access to information and statistics on how well past graduates from your high school have done at his or her college. In addition, if you attended a larger, or well-known, high school, the college will likely have assigned an admissions officer to your school, and they will have a very accurate knowledge of exactly what your high school has to offer.

Today, most high schools will attach to your transcript a profile describing courses offered, grading systems, and other vital statistics. This profile will allow the admissions officer a better insight as to the curriculum offered at your high school. This information is especially helpful for the college's admissions officer if he or she has no other way of researching your high school's history.

The strength of your high school is, in most cases, beyond your control, and actually has very little bearing on your acceptance to a particular college, given the fact you are an average to above average student. In the event your admission decision is borderline, the strength (or track record) of your high school could be very instrumental in putting your application for admission over the top.

PSAT, SAT, and ACT testing

Most colleges today require either the ACT or SAT test as a pre-requisite for admission. The majority of the colleges across the country will accept both, but one of the two is required before your application for admission is made.

These two tests are designed to measure the student's aptitude for college-level work and the student's achievements in a variety of subjects.

The SAT test may be taken more than once. In fact, it is recommended that the student take the SAT at least two times, possibly three, due to the fact that the college will usually only look at the highest score when determining the student's eligibility for enrollment.

In addition to the SAT is the *SAT II*, which are subject tests given on particular areas such as math, English, and science. These tests should also be taken because they will give the admissions officer a look at your true strengths in a particular subject.

The *PSAT* is a preparatory test for the SAT and should be taken in the student's high school sophomore or junior year. The PSAT will help determine the student's eligibility for the National Merit Scholarship as well as prepare him/her to take the SAT.

Activities and community involvement

Colleges want to see students who are active in both school and community activities. It is important that you not only join a club or participate in an activity, but you must be active in what you choose to join. Colleges are much more concerned with quality, when it comes to activities by the student, than quantity.

> E-Z TIP
> Colleges are looking for students who show interests in two or three specific activities and focus on those.

Students who jump from club to club and activity to activity, without any real commitment or participation, are not what the colleges are looking for. A student who has an entire list of clubs and/or activities, with no real participation in any, is often referred to as a person who is "padding his/her resume." This "padding" can prove very costly when it comes to the college making its acceptance decision.

It is far better to pick two or three areas of interest and be an active member of each. A few examples are as follows:

- Math club
- Foreign language club

- Science Club
- Scouting
- Volunteer groups and organizations in the community

Whatever group or organization you choose, you must be active. If you are going to be in an activity, make the most out of it. Find something that truly interests you and stick with it. It will help you both as a person, and also will go a great distance toward your acceptance by a college or university.

The college's admissions officer needs to be able to see that you genuinely make a difference in your community by your involvement and active participation. The admissions officer will be anxious to have a student with that type of character on campus.

This chapter has outlined for you what you should be aware of when making your high school preparations for college. In addition, it has covered what the colleges are looking for in their applicants. Planning ahead and getting your high school transcript in order is one of the most important things you can do while still in high school. Building a solid foundation by following the steps outlined in this chapter will pay off great rewards down the line. It takes work. In fact, work is the key. Remember that the entire college selection, preparation, and funding process will take a great deal of time, energy, and effort. It will all be well worth it. Remember that you are investing in your education, your goals, and your future. You are investing in yourself.

Chapter 5

SAT and ACT testing

What you'll find in this chapter:

- Analysis and preparation for the SAT
- Analysis and preparation for the SAT II
- When and how to take the SAT and SAT II
- Analysis and preparation for the ACT
- How often to test

This chapter is divided into two sections; the first contains information regarding the SAT and the second, obviously, is dedicated to the ACT. These tests are both accepted by most all colleges and universities across the country as admissions examinations, and share many similarities. These two tests also have a few distinct differences.

It is recommended that the student take both tests and compare the scores from each to see which will better portray the student's strengths to the colleges to which they are making admission applications. It is also recommended that the student take these tests more than once. The timeline in Chapter 2 recommends taking the test during both the student's high school junior and senior year. The student may actually take each test twice, compare and find the best scores and submit those results to the colleges.

> **HOT spot** Over half of the students who took these tests more than once increased their scores with the second exam.

In addition, testing more than once is recommended because colleges and universities that see students taking multiple tests look favorably on the student's interest and desire to succeed in life. This could have an effect on the institution when it comes to offering the student admission.

DEFINITION

The SAT also offers a pre-test called the *PSAT*. This is an excellent way for the student to gain confidence and knowledge pertaining to the SAT. The student may take the PSAT during their high school sophomore year, and like the SAT, this test may be taken more than one time for additional practice.

SAT

The SAT is actually made up of two separate types of tests, the SAT I and the SAT II.

The *SAT I* is designed to measure the student's verbal and math reasoning ability skills. These are abilities that are developed over time through work the student does in school and on his/her own. The SAT I scores help the colleges better understand how the student compares with the other student applicants who are preparing for college.

DEFINITION

The *SAT II* are one-hour subject tests, which are primarily multiple-choice and deal with specific subjects. These tests measure the student's knowledge and/or skills in a particular subject and the student's ability to apply that knowledge. Many colleges require and/or recommend one or more of the subject tests for admission. The institutions commonly use this information in combination with the student's high school record and recommendation letters to determine eligibility for enrollment. The SAT II often provide a dependable measure of the student's academic achievement and are a good predictor of the student's future performance.

SAT I

There are two basic types of questions on the SAT I:

1) Verbal questions, which include:

- ✧ Analogy questions which measure the students:
    - knowledge of the meaning of words
    - ability to see a relationship between pairs of words
    - ability to recognize a similar or parallel relationship
- ✧ Sentence completion questions which measure:
    - knowledge of the meaning of words
    - ability to understand how the different parts of a sentence logically fit together
- ✧ Critical reading questions which measure ability to read and think carefully about a single reading passage or a pair of related passages

2) Math questions, which include the following subjects:

- ✧ Arithmetic
- ✧ Algebra
- ✧ Geometry
- ✧ Logical reasoning

Calculators are permitted and, in fact, recommended when taking the SAT I. Research has shown that students who use calculators often test better than those students who do not. These calculators must be basic four-function, scientific, or graphing calculators. No hand-held mini computers, pocket organizers, calculators with paper tape, or any similar devices are permitted. Also, sharing of calculators is not permitted.

Preparation for the SAT I

> note
>
> Research has proven that students who have taken more academic courses and who have earned good grades often get higher SAT scores than those students with fewer academic courses and lower grades.

It is strongly recommended that the students challenge themselves all through high school by taking as many academic courses as can be managed. By enrolling and working hard at these courses, the student will definitely see the payoffs when it comes to testing and the college admission process.

Tips on how to test effectively

The following tips are designed to help the student do his/her best on the SAT:

- Learn the test directions ahead of time. The amount of time you spend reading and interpreting the directions during the testing time will take away from the time you have to answer the test questions. It is important to know the directions prior to the test date.

- Do the easier questions first. You earn the same amount of points for all questions. Complete the easier ones first and then go back to the more complicated ones.

- If you are forced to guess, be sure to guess smart. Most generally there will be questions that the student simply doesn't know the answer to and will be forced to guess. By ruling out one or more answers in a multiple-choice question, the chances of guessing the right answer greatly increase.

- Do not panic if you are not able to answer every question. You do not have to answer every question correctly to get a high score.

- Quickly omit any questions that you simply have no idea of how to answer. Keep in mind that there are no points lost for an omitted question and you shouldn't spend time on a question that you have no idea how to answer. Finish the rest of the test and then come back to the most difficult questions during your final review.

- Be careful when filling out the answer sheet grids. Some questions are multiple-choice and some are not; double-check to make sure that your answers are transposed to the answer grid sheet correctly and accurately.

- Do not make any extra marks on the answer sheet. A machine will score all the answer sheets, and the machine will not be able to determine the difference between an answer and a scribble on the page. Reserve the answer sheet grid for the answers only.

- Be sure to mark only one answer per multiple-choice question. Marking more than one is a common mistake and you should double-check to prevent this mistake from happening.

- Taking the PSAT is an excellent way to practice for the SAT I. The PSAT is a shorter test with the same sort of questions as the SAT I and will be an excellent way for the student to prepare.

SAT II

The SAT II is designed to give the colleges and universities an idea of the student's knowledge or skill level in a particular subject. This also gives the institution an impression of how the student may apply knowledge.

The SAT II tests are available for the following subjects:

- English
  - ✧ Writing
  - ✧ Literature
- History
  - ✧ World history
  - ✧ American history and social studies
- Science
  - ✧ Chemistry
  - ✧ Biology
  - ✧ Physics
- Mathematics
  - ✧ Mathematics level IC
  - ✧ Mathematics level IIC

- Language (reading only)
    - ✧ German
    - ✧ French
    - ✧ Italian
    - ✧ Modern Hebrew
    - ✧ Latin
    - ✧ Spanish
- Language (listening)
    - ✧ French
    - ✧ German
    - ✧ Chinese
    - ✧ Japanese
    - ✧ Korean
    - ✧ Spanish
    - ✧ English language proficiency

When to take the SAT II

E-Z TIP

Due to the fact that the SAT II testing programs cover specific subjects (such as chemistry, physics, history, biology, language, etc.), it is best to carefully plan your testing dates to coincide with the particular courses for which you are testing. For example, it is better to test for biology, chemistry, physics, and American history as soon as their related high school courses end. This will allow students to take the test while the information is still fresh in their minds. Likewise, it is best to take the writing and language tests after the student has had several years studying on those particular subjects.

Calculators

Calculators are permitted, in fact recommended, for certain SAT II testing. The stipulations for calculator type and use are the same as for the SAT I test, which were listed earlier in this chapter. Below is a list of tips that the student may wish to consider regarding the use of a calculator:

- Some of the test questions require a calculator. To take the test without one would surely put the student at a disadvantage.

- Use a calculator that you are familiar with; taking unnecessary time to discover the workings of your calculator could be very costly.

- Because there will be no calculators, or substitute calculators, available to the student at the testing center, it is important to make sure your calculator is in good working condition (with a new battery) prior to the testing date.

- Remember that not all questions on the test require the use of a calculator.

- Before using the calculator, determine if one is needed for each particular question by first thinking through how you will solve the problem. Then decide whether a calculator will be necessary to arrive at the answer.

- There is no sharing of a calculator. Any sharing will be automatic grounds for dismissal from the test with no score.

Tips for the SAT II test

Below is a list of tips and ideas that may help you test more effectively when taking the SAT II. Although the student may incorporate some of the same tips listed in the SAT I section earlier in this chapter, there are also a couple of added tips listed below that refer directly to the SAT II:

- Knowing when to take each subject test is important. There are basically two types of subject tests. One you should take while the information is still fresh in your mind, such as biology, chemistry, and world history. And the other type can be better taken after the student has had a few years to study and accumulate knowledge regarding that specific subject, such as a language test.

- Know the test directions and what to expect ahead of time. By preparing for the test prior to the testing day, the student will have more time during the testing session to concentrate on the answers and not have to worry about the rules, directions, etc.

- Always do the easiest questions first and then come back to the more difficult ones. Remember that you can earn as many points for a correct answer on an easy question as you can on a more difficult one.

- Knowing how the tests are scored is very beneficial. The student gets one point for each correct answer and loses a fraction of a point for each wrong answer. The student neither gains nor loses a point for a question they omitted. The procedure should then be to answer the easier questions first, then the next easiest, and save the hardest for last. Omitting one of the hard questions will not count against the student.

Registering for the SAT I and the SAT II

To register for the PSAT, SAT I, and/or the SAT II the student may wish to inquire with their high school guidance counselor's office. The student will need to ask their counselor for the Registration Bulletin, which will include a Registration Form and return envelope. The Registration Bulletin also includes test dates, registration deadlines, fees, instructions, test center codes, and other registration-related information.

In addition, the student may also contact the SAT through the College Board Online web-site, which is located at www.sat.org

The student may also write to the College Board SAT Program at: P.O. Box 6200, Princeton, NJ 08541-6200, or call them at (609) 771-7600. Their office hours are Monday through Friday from 8 a.m. to 8:45 p.m., Eastern Time.

Re-registration for the SAT I and SAT II

If you are a high school student who has previously registered for a SAT I and/or a SAT II test, you can call SAT directly and re-register by phone at (609) 771-7600, or toll free (800) 728-7267. These numbers are accessible 24 hours a day, 7 days a week and require that you use a touch-tone phone, a credit card for payment, and require no additional customer service—other than to re-register.

If you need additional assistance, you may speak with a customer service representative by calling (609) 771-7600, Monday through Friday between the hours of 8 a.m. and 8:45 p.m., Eastern Time. When calling you will be asked for the following information:

- Your name, date of birth, sex, social security number
- To register for SAT II—you will need to know the two-digit test codes
- The five-digit test center codes
- The four-digit college or scholarship codes
- Visa, MasterCard, or American Express number and month and year of expiration

If you are unsure of the codes which are required and listed above, you will be able to locate them at the SAT's web-site or ask your high school guidance counselor.

Scores and reporting

Your score report will be mailed to you approximately three weeks after your original test date. In addition, if you requested that your score(s) be sent to colleges and/or scholarship sponsors, a report will also be sent to them within three weeks after you have taken the test.

If you have not received your test score report within eight weeks from your original test date, you should contact SAT and check the status of your results. In your correspondences you should include your name, date of birth, mailing address, test date, and registration number (if available).

The day of the test

Plan to arrive at the test center between 8:00 and 8:15 a.m. on the day of the test. Testing usually starts at around 8:30 a.m. and generally runs until 12:30 p.m. The testing time allows for a short break every hour.

If you are taking the SAT I, you must work within each section of the test only for the time allotted. You will not be permitted to go back to a section once that section has ended, nor will you be permitted to go ahead to finish a section early. The testing supervisor will guide you through the testing process and provide you with all the necessary instructions.

ACT

The ACT assessment is a national college admission examination that consists of tests in:

- English
- Reading
- Mathematics
- Science Reasoning

The ACT offers a comprehensive way for high school students to demonstrate to the colleges and universities to which they are applying that they can become successful college students. Virtually every college and university in the country accepts the ACT test and its results.

The ACT includes 215 multiple-choice questions and takes approximately three and one-half hours to complete (including breaks). In the United States, the ACT is offered on five separate national test dates, in October, December, February, April, and June. In a few selected states, the ACT is also offered in late September. For the 1999-2000 school year the basic registration fee for the SAT is $22, which includes reports of the student's scores to four different colleges and/or universities.

The highest possible score on the ACT is 36, with the national average score being 21. The ACT assessment program was founded in 1959 and is available in all 50 states. There are currently over 1.7 million ACT assessments administered each year.

The ACT assessment is curriculum based. It is not an aptitude or an IQ test. Instead, the questions on the ACT are directly related to what the student has learned in high school English, mathematics, and science courses.

Because ACT tests are based on what the students are taught in high school, students are generally more comfortable with the ACT than they are with traditional aptitude tests.

The ACT assessment is actually more than a test. It also provides test takers with a unique interest inventory that contains valuable information for career and educational planning, and a student profile section that provides a comprehensive profile of the student's high school work and future plans.

When to test

As outlined in the timeline, which is contained in Chapter 2, the student should take the ACT (and the SAT as well, if possible) in February of the high school junior year, and then again during the senior year.

It is recommended to take the ACT and SAT tests more than one time. Most students will show an improvement in the scores of their second test, and they may submit the higher results to the colleges and universities with the admission applications.

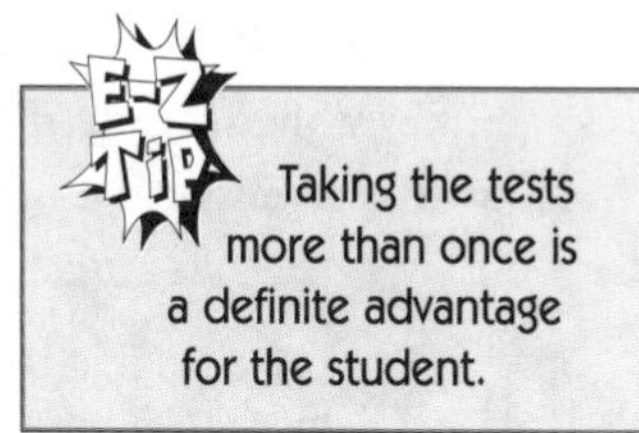

E-Z TIP
Taking the tests more than once is a definite advantage for the student.

There are several other advantages to testing early (during your high school junior year):

- You will have test results and scores in time to make a difference in your senior year courses. For example, if you show a weakness in a particular area of the test you may wish to take an additional class to give you more strength in that particular area before retaking the ACT test (and SAT, if possible) during your senior year.

- Colleges and universities typically receive the names of students who test. These institutions then begin sending the students information regarding their particular school. By testing in the high school junior year, the student will begin receiving this information sooner and, consequently, have more time to evaluate each college's material.

- Testing during your high school junior year will give you that all-important chance to retest. Remember that your first test may have been taken on a day that you didn't feel 100 percent, or were nervous, and you would hate for that to reflect negatively on your chances for admission to a particular college or university.

How often can a student retest and which scores are reported if the student tests more than once?

The student may take the ACT assessment as often as he/she wishes. However, the majority of students follow the recommendations of testing twice, once during their high school junior year and once during their senior year. ACT research does show that more than half of the students who test a second time increase their composite scores.

> **HOT spot** If a student tests more than once (as recommended), the student controls which scores are sent to the colleges and universities.

ACT maintains a separate record for each individual testing session and will send only the scores to the colleges and universities from the date you choose. This will protect the student and ensure that he/she will maintain control of his/her records.

Results of the tests are normally mailed to the student about four weeks after the test date. In order to keep all scores confidential, they will not be given out to anyone by fax, telephone, or e-mail.

How to contact ACT/registration

To register for the ACT assessment you may wish to inquire with your high school guidance counselor's office. In addition, you may also contact the ACT through their web-site, which is located at *www.act.org*. The student may also write to ACT Registration at: P.O. Box 414, Iowa City, IA 52243-0414, or call them at (319) 337-1270. Their office hours are Monday through Friday from 8 a.m. to 8:00 p.m., Central Time.

How to change test center assignments and/or dates

If you should need to change your test center location, or your test date, call ACT at (319) 337-1270. You must contact ACT no later than the late deadline, which you have been given. You must have your social security number, your test date, your code number for your preferred test center, and your credit card ready when contacting ACT to change the test date or location.

note

If there is room at your preferred test center on your new test date, you will be assigned to that center and your credit card will be charged. In the event the preferred test center is full on the date you requested, you will not be able to make the desired change.

Important information for students with disabilities

If you are a student who currently receives accommodations in school due to a professionally diagnosed and documented disability, you may be entitled to certain testing center options. To determine your eligibility for these options you may wish to contact ACT directly at (319) 337-1332, and ask for their "Request of ACT Assessment Special Testing."

Homebound students

If you are a homebound student, or confined to a hospital on scheduled test dates, do not register. Instead, write to ACT Universal Testing at: P.O. Box 4028, Iowa City, IA 52243-4028, and describe your circumstances. ACT will send you information regarding "Arranged Testing."

Score reports

To receive information on the status of score reports, delayed or missing reports, or a score report correction, you may contact the office of ACT Records at: P.O. Box 451, Iowa City, IA 52243-0451, or telephone them at (319) 337-1313. Their business hours are Monday through Friday, from 8:30 a.m. to 4:30 p.m., central time.

This office will not release any information regarding the student's test results or original scores. Due to confidentiality, this information is only released through direct mail to the student and institutions which the student has authorized to receive the information.

What to bring the day of the test

We have compiled a list of important items that you will need to take with you the day of your ACT test. Please be sure to bring all of these items to the testing center with you:

- Your test center admission ticket.

- Acceptable and/or appropriate identification. Remember that your admission ticket is not identification. You will need to bring an appropriate form of picture identification with you, such as a driver's license, passport, or school identification card, in order to test. Unfortunately, if you do not have the proper identification, you will not be allowed to take the ACT.

- Three sharpened number 2 pencils with erasers. Highlighting pens, or similar written instruments, are not permitted in the testing center. Bring only pencils.

- A wristwatch, if you wish to keep time and pace your progress while testing. The testing supervisor will announce when there is five minutes remaining in each testing session.

- A calculator for completion of the Mathematics portion of the test. Acceptable calculators are covered earlier in this chapter.

E-Z TIP Be sure you know the exact location of the testing center and the best way to get there. If you are unsure of the location or the most accessible route, take the time to drive by the center prior to testing day and plan your course so there will be no confusion on the day of the test.

Preparing for the testing day

Take the time to study the instructions, follow all directions carefully, and be sure to take the practice test that is included in the free booklet you will receive upon registration, *Preparing for the ACT Assessment.*

E-Z TIP
It is vital to read all the information contained in your registration packet prior to arriving at the testing location.

Be sure to get plenty of rest the night before the ACT test. A clear, rested mind will go a long ways toward testing successfully. You should also plan on eating a breakfast that will give you the energy you need for four hours of intense concentration. In addition, you should dress comfortably while taking the ACT. Remember that some test centers may be warmer and/or colder than others and it is a good idea to wear layered clothing so that you will be comfortable no matter what conditions you encounter.

Tips for successful ACT testing

By far the best preparation a student can have for the ACT is taking solid high school courses such as English, math, social studies and science. The student must not only enroll in these courses; he/she must take them seriously, study hard, and effectively apply himself/herself.

It is important that the student begin preparing for the ACT early, and the best way to do this is by preparing with a challenging high school curriculum.

Here are a few general tips for successful testing:

- Carefully read all the instructions on the cover of the test booklet.
- Read and understand the specific directions for each individual test section.

- ✧ The English, reading, and science reasoning tests ask for the best answer. Be sure to read all answers before you choose the one that best responds to the question.

- ✧ The mathematics test asks only for the correct answer. Read each and every question carefully to make sure you understand the type of answer that is required.

• Read all questions carefully.

• Pace yourself. The time limits given provide practically everyone with enough time to answer all the questions. However, some tests do include reading passages. Do not spend too much time on a single passage and/or any one question contained in the test.

• Answer the easiest questions first.

• Answer the toughest questions next, by using logic and the process of elimination. For example, if you simply don't know the answer to a specific question (and that will happen), you should eliminate as many incorrect answers as you can, then make an educated guess among the remaining choices.

• Be sure to answer every question. Unlike the SAT test there is no penalty for answering a question incorrectly. It is to your definite advantage on the ACT to answer every question on the test.

• Always review your work. If you finish your test prior to the allotted time limit, go back and check your work and/or answers to all the questions which you have time to review.

HOT spot ACT bases its score on your number of correct answers, and makes no deduction for wrong answers. Be sure to answer every question on the exam.

- Mark your answers neatly.

- If you must erase an answer, make sure you erase it neatly and completely before you make the corrected answer notation.

Chapter 6

The college search & selection process

What you'll find in this chapter:

- Compiling your list of possible colleges
- Researching and narrowing your list
- Reducing your list to six colleges
- Arranging your finalists in proper order

One of the most important decisions involved in obtaining a college education and degree is obviously selecting the most suitable college. It must be a college where the student will excel and achieve. It must be a place where the student feels comfortable. The average student spends five years at the selected college; you should spend the time necessary to make absolutely sure you have picked the right college for you. The college you select is undoubtedly going to have the biggest influence on your future. Please, do so cautiously and carefully—this will be one of the biggest and most important decisions of your life. This chapter will outline the procedures for effective evaluation and determination of possible colleges that would be best suited for your future educational needs.

> **HOT spot** Parents are surely advisers, and the student should welcome their advice, but selecting the right college must be the student's final decision.

Only the student can choose the best all-around college. Your parents cannot make the decision for you. Again, they can only advise.

E-Z TIP
The student must look for a college that is right for himself/herself—not for friends or family.

You should always identify schools you want to go to and then look for the financial aid. Don't rule out any college; not even those that cost in excess of $25,000 per year, because you think you can't afford the cost of attendance. The financial aid portion of the college preparation process is covered in great detail later in this guidebook. It is important to know and remember that the entire college preparation, selection, application, and financial aid process is a highly sequential procedure and must be approached with that in mind. The amount you pay for your education may be about the same no matter which college you eventually select if all the steps (outlined in this guidebook) in the college preparation and funding process are followed closely.

> **HOT spot** When you *start* your search for the ideal college, money should not even be your primary consideration.

The college selection process is actually divided into three separate parts, which include:

1) Compiling your original list of colleges that interest you based on specific criteria (size, location, etc.). This list should contain between 20 and 30 colleges, maybe more.

2) Narrowing your list of possible colleges to between eight and ten by doing further research into the original list of institutions you selected.

3) Finally, cutting the list to six finalist colleges. From this list of six you will be able to do further research by visiting the college's campuses, etc. to determine which is the most appealing to you. You will then be able to arrange your six finalists in the following order:

a) Your top four choices, in order

b) A "long shot" selection

c) A safety valve selection

The entire college selection process should actually begin in the second semester of your high school sophomore year and continue into the fall of your senior year. The earlier you get started and the more time you have to research the college's information, the more informed decision you will be able to make.

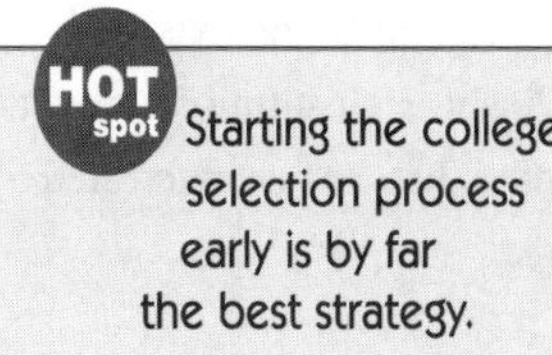

HOT
spot
Starting the college selection process early is by far the best strategy.

We realize that everyone is not able to start his or her college search in the sophomore year of high school. Those who start their search later should devote additional time to the college search and selection part of the college preparation process in order to have the most information available to make the most informed decision.

In this chapter we will cover, in detail, the three parts of the college search and selection process. You will learn how to start your original list, narrow your choices, and ultimately trim your selections to six finalists. You will receive hints, tips, ideas, and strategies for locating the most attractive colleges based on your personal goals and desires. We will show you where to do your research, how to compare your findings, and how to arrive at a final decision.

This chapter, along with the entire guidebook, is not intended to influence your decisions while preparing for college in any way, shape, or form. We are simply outlining procedures (based on proven methods and results) which you may follow, that may help you by saving you time and money. We realize that the college preparation and funding process is confusing, and by putting our strategies and step-by-step procedures to use, hopefully any indecision you may have will be eliminated. In addition, we hope the information you gather from this guidebook will assist you in making the most informed decisions possible. We trust that the strategies and ideas outlined in this chapter, and this guidebook, will help you a great deal; however, remember that the final decisions will ultimately be yours.

Compiling your original list of possible colleges

Your original list of possible colleges should range somewhere between 20 and 30 institutions, maybe more. You may have a few schools in mind right now that you are interested in, and they should definitely be included in your list.

There are two effective methods of compiling your original list of possible colleges by obtaining the college's specifics and statistical profiles:

First, you may visit your library and review a college directory, or you may purchase your own college directory, which are available in most bookstores. These directories will have listings for all the accredited colleges and universities in the country. The college directories contain information on over 3,200 accredited institutions, such as: enrollment size, location, majors, costs, ratio of students to professors, percentage of students who receive financial aid, percentage of financial aid that is gift aid in relationship to self-help aid, and much more.

The college directory may also be used for other steps in the college preparation and funding process, such as Chapters 10 and 11, regarding the sources of, and applying for, financial aid, and Chapters 14 and 15, evaluating and negotiating the college's financial aid award packages.

HOT spot A good quality college directory may be a wise investment to make; it may actually be used as a reference source through the entire college preparation and funding process.

Second, if you have access to the Internet, you may wish to use the "free" on-line college searches that are now available. These searches allow you to enter the criteria you are looking for in a college and will then provide you with a list of institutions that meet those criteria. We have listed two of the top "free" college searches that are available:

1) The College Net, which is located at *www.collegenet.com*

2) The College Locator, which is located at *www.ecola.com/college*

When using either the college directories or the on-line college search services, to compile your original list of potential colleges, it is important to keep three things in mind:

1) You are not trying to find the perfect college. The perfect college probably does not exist; however, there are more than 3,200 accredited colleges and universities across the country, and several of those campuses may be right for you in their own way.

2) Do not take money into consideration when compiling your original list of 20 to 30 possible colleges. We will cover the financial aid portion of the process later in this guidebook, where you will receive strategies and ideas that will hopefully allow you to receive the college degree you desire at the institution of your choice without worrying about funding. This should be a college where you will be able to excel as a student and as a person, and money should not be taken into consideration while making that decision.

Financial aid will obviously be a big part of your final college choice selection; we will cover later in the guidebook how to incorporate financial aid package information into your final college choice decision.

HOT spot Money for college is available, but first you need to determine which is the best college for you.

3) The final college choice decision must be the student's. Although parents are advisors, the student needs to make the final decision on which college to attend.

Beginning your search

There are basically two top criteria to consider when compiling your original list of 20 to 30 possible colleges:

1) How strong is the school's program in the field you have chosen to study?

2) How closely does the campus fit your desires for size, location, and distance from home?

Keep in mind your original list of 20 to 30 possible colleges will later be narrowed down to six finalist schools. Plan to visit each campus of the six finalists (campus visits are covered in detail in Chapter 12) in order to obtain more information that will help you with your final college choice selection.

During these campus visits there are three more specific areas that you should consider:

1) What impression did you get from the students and the entire college community?

2) Are the professors and staff receptive, and would they be the kind of people you enjoy working with?

3) Can you picture yourself as a part of the college community?

The college campus visits are covered in detail in Chapter 12, and should start after your list of possible colleges is narrowed down to six finalists.

Below is a list of basic information that will give you an idea of what parameters you will have to choose from when doing your college searches. You should review and familiarize yourself with all of these in order to get a feel for what type of institution you are searching for:

- Type of institution
  - ✧ public
  - ✧ private
  - ✧ secular
  - ✧ Private and Catholic, Jewish, or Protestant
- Enrollment size
  - ✧ below 1000
  - ✧ 1000 —2000
  - ✧ 2000 —3000
  - ✧ 3000 —5000
  - ✧ 5000 —10,000
  - ✧ above 10,000
- College setting
  - ✧ rural
  - ✧ small town
  - ✧ large town

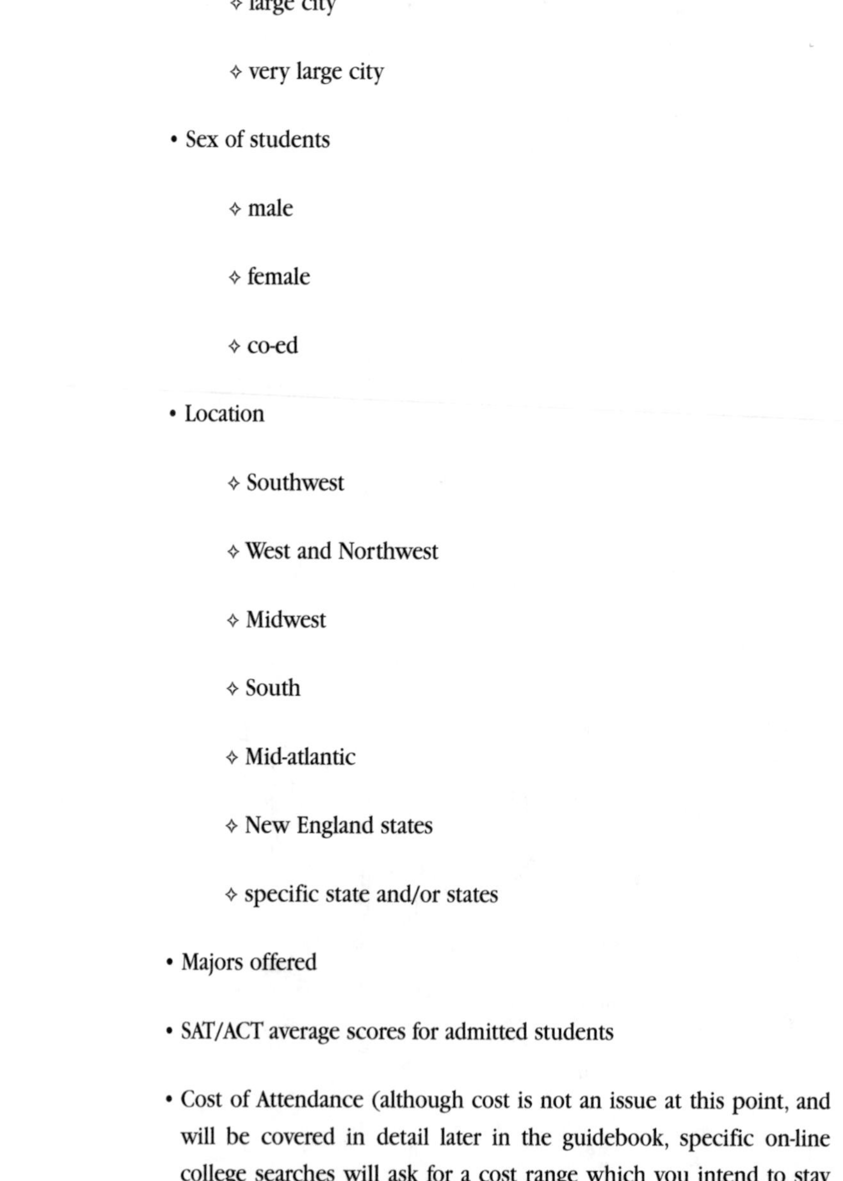

  - small city
  - large city
  - very large city
- Sex of students
  - male
  - female
  - co-ed
- Location
  - Southwest
  - West and Northwest
  - Midwest
  - South
  - Mid-atlantic
  - New England states
  - specific state and/or states
- Majors offered
- SAT/ACT average scores for admitted students
- Cost of Attendance (although cost is not an issue at this point, and will be covered in detail later in the guidebook, specific on-line college searches will ask for a cost range which you intend to stay

within. Simply check all ranges and the search will return results from all colleges that meet your other criteria, regardless of their total cost of enrollment.)

From the information listed above you will be able to run a preliminary search, either by computer or by using a college directory. You may run this search by state or by region.

After running your original college search, you should begin a file with your findings. This file should include all information you gather on each individual institution. Often, the computer-driven college searches will have links available to take you directly to the college's web page, which will have an enormous amount of information regarding the college. You may wish to print out some of this information (enrollment size, location, addresses, phone numbers, cost of education, requirements for admission, etc.) and include it in the college's file.

Obtaining the college's address and phone number during the college search process may prove to be very helpful. If the college eventually makes your original list of 20-30 possible institutions, you will be writing them for additional information to do further research and having their address will save you a great deal of time and effort.

When compiling your original list of 20 to 30 institutions, be sure to include any colleges that you may already have in mind.

College search services

There are companies available that offer a college search program for a fee. Their information is often on a CD-Rom or videotape. One question we commonly hear from students and parents is, "Should we hire a company to do the college search for us?" The answer to that is obviously up to the student and the parents; however, here are a couple of things to consider before hiring a college search company:

- The college search service is usually not a search at all. The colleges and universities advertised on the CDs and/or videotapes have usually paid for the exposure. This is actually a form of advertising for the institutions and not a true search for your specific criteria.

- You may run a "free" college search through the Internet and the World Wide Web. This search will contain the exact criteria you request and will return the matches that fit your educational needs.

Running the search & narrowing your list

We will now give you an example of a high school student searching for the best college. We will follow her through the entire search and selection process, from how to create the original list, to writing the schools for additional information, to narrowing her list down to six finalists. A reminder: This is only an example and although the process you may follow is much the same, your numbers will undoubtedly be different.

HOT spot Remember you will spend four years of your life at the institution you choose. Therefore, you must spend the time necessary to make absolutely sure of your selection.

Pay close attention to the time frame which our student follows during the college search and selection process. Timing is vital. The process does require work.

The hypothetical student, Michelle, is a high school sophomore who is preparing for college. She is taking the necessary and required courses. She has taken the PSAT test and will be taking the SAT soon. She will be taking advanced placement courses later in her high school career. She has decided on a general area of study, and now she needs to begin her college search to eventually locate the college that will best suit her future educational needs. Michelle has specific requirements she will be looking for in a college. Michelle also knows the college search process will take time; however, she is willing to spend the necessary time because she is anxious to invest in her college education and her future in any way that she can.

Michelle is now in her second sophomore semester and has developed a real interest in math. In addition, Michelle has aspired to be a teacher for years, and has made the decision to pursue a career as a math teacher. Michelle will begin her search for colleges based on other criteria (size, location, etc.), but she knows that she will also need a college or university that offers majors in both teaching and mathematics.

Enrollment size and location

Michelle has specific parameters in mind. She would like to go to a middle-sized school (an enrollment of fewer than 5,000) within a four-state area of her hometown. Michelle begins her original search on her home computer and goes to one of the free college searches that are available over the World Wide Web. She puts the specifics of enrollment size and location into the search and as a result gets a list of 71 possible colleges in her four-state area.

Specialized schools

Of these 71 colleges, Michelle notices that 21 of them are specialized schools (institutes, nursing schools, etc.). Since an institution like this does not appeal to Michelle, she deducts these schools from her list and now has 50 schools remaining.

Michelle then goes directly to the colleges' web-sites and gathers more detailed information regarding the 50 remaining schools.

On-campus housing

By purchasing a college directory and doing further research, Michelle finds that eight of the 50 colleges offer no on-campus housing. Since Michelle wishes to live on-campus, she deducts these eight institutions from her list and is now left with 42 possibilities.

This research takes time. In fact, Michelle has spent many hours over the past two months researching, making notes and determinations of possible colleges. Michelle now sets this list of 42 possibilities aside for a while and takes a break from the search process.

During her break from the college search process, Michelle will receive, and should take the time to review, unsolicited information in the mail from several colleges and universities. One of these brochures may catch Michelle's eye and a few of them may even be from colleges that Michelle has included in her list of 42 remaining possibilities. While taking a break from the list of 42, Michelle and her parents attend a college fair to get a feel for what the colleges have to offer and hopefully gather additional information regarding her current list of schools. Michelle gathers some additional information that she feels may be helpful in narrowing her list and includes the information in her files.

Minimum enrollment

At the beginning of Michelle's high school junior year she begins to narrow her list of 42 down even farther. By talking with friends, parents, her guidance counselor, and a few other people, she has determined that she really does not want to attend a very small school (under an enrollment of 1,000). Michelle then goes back to her list and finds that eight of the 42 remaining schools have an enrollment of fewer than 1,000 so she eliminates those from the list, leaving 34 schools.

Type of enrolled students

Michelle then notices that five of the schools have single-sex enrollment, and since she would like to attend an institution with a balanced enrollment, Michelle deducts the five from the 34 and now has her list down to 29 possible colleges.

College degrees offered

The final (and maybe most important) item that Michelle must take into consideration in narrowing her list is if each institution offers majors in her expected area of study, math and teaching. Michelle again refers to the college directories and sees that only 21 of the 29 remaining colleges offer degrees in both math and teaching.

Michelle has now successfully trimmed her list of possible colleges down to 21. It has taken some time and effort; however, with a plan of action and organization, Michelle has been able to effectively locate 21 colleges in the four-state area surrounding her hometown that fit her criteria for furthering her education.

Writing for information

After narrowing her list to 21 colleges, Michelle is ready for the next step, which is writing to each individual college or university that she has listed to request all available information regarding the institution.

Michelle does this immediately after completing her list by writing to the admissions office of each institution and requesting any information that would be pertinent to her decision-making process; essentially, any information they would be willing to send. In Michelle's letter she also tells them a little bit about herself, including her interests, her probable area of study, along with a few of her talents. Michelle uses a computer to personalize each letter. This also saves time and, in addition, a personalized letter always makes a better impression on the person who receives it.

We have included for you a sample information request letter that may be used when writing to the colleges on your list:

Today 1, 2000

Mr. John E. Select
Dean of Admissions
ABC University
123 4th Street
Atlanta, GA 12345-6789

Dear Dean Select:

I am a junior at XYZ High School in Big Town, USA, and I am seeking information on specific colleges that might fit my educational needs after graduation. Your institution, due to its size and location, as well as majors in education, is on my list of colleges under consideration.

Please send me all relative information that may assist me with my decision, such as: admission requirements, courses available, financial aid, and campus housing. Feel free to include any additional information that you feel may help me.

I would like to thank you in advance for your time and your help.

Sincerely,
I M Student

High school counselor and further research

While Michelle is waiting to hear from the colleges from which she has requested information, she continues to do further research by again talking with her high school counselor.

The high school counselor often has good information, and possibly a couple of ideas and suggestions that would make your college selection search more effective.

HINT

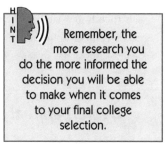

Remember, the more research you do the more informed the decision you will be able to make when it comes to your final college selection.

In addition to speaking with her high school counselor, Michelle also continues to read and review the unsolicited mail she receives from assorted colleges. If a college's material appeals to Michelle, she may wish to do further research on the institution and eventually include it in her list of 21 remaining college possibilities.

When Michelle starts receiving the requested information from the 21 colleges and universities she wrote to, and starts evaluating each college further, she creates a file for each institution. These files will prove very valuable for future reference. Michelle tries to get a general feel for the institution, by reviewing its enrollment requirements, number of students, etc.

Narrowing the list—Eight to ten semi-finalists

By the end of her first semester of her high school junior year Michelle should have received and reviewed enough information from the colleges, as well as done enough research, to now narrow her list of colleges down to between eight and 10 semifinalists.

HOT spot

Remember, your goal is to make the most informed decision possible, and in order to do this you will need the greatest amount of information available.

In order to narrow her list to these semifinalists, Michelle will need to gather all the information possible and do in-depth research on each institution. Michelle continues to talk with friends and family, past graduates from the institutions, and her high school counselor. In fact, she makes an effort to visit with anyone who Michelle thinks has information or an opinion on one of the institutions on her list.

Overall appeal

By now, Michelle is able to rule out 11 schools due to the fact that through her further research she has found nothing that makes these institutions stand out. By deducting these 11 schools, Michelle now has a semi-finalist list of ten remaining schools.

Reducing the list to six finalists

Enrollment minimum

It is now early in Michelle's high school senior year and it is time for her to cut her list from 10 semi-finalists down to six finalists. Michelle has discovered that two of the 10 semi-finalist schools have enrollments of around 1,100, which is too close to the minimum number of students preferred by Michelle, so she takes those two off the list and is now left with eight.

Campus reputations

In addition, Michelle has discovered from her conversations with friends and family that two of the colleges have bad reputations for crime and other related actions. After Michelle eliminates these two schools from consideration and deducts them from her list, she is now left with her six finalist colleges.

Although it has taken Michelle hours of research and a great deal of effort, she has successfully narrowed her list of possible colleges down to six finalists. By organizing her information well and sticking with her plan of action, she was able to compile a list of the six colleges that would best suit her future educational needs.

note

Please remember that Michelle's situation was created; however, this is typically the procedure to be followed when compiling a list of possible colleges. Again, your numbers will surely vary because of different parameters, regions of the country, etc. By following the general overall principles we have outlined in the example of Michelle's search, you will be able to make effective use of your time and also create your own list of schools that may be right for you.

After your list is narrowed from the hundreds of possible colleges and universities down to six finalists, you will be ready for the next step in the college selection process, the college campus visits, which is covered in detail in Chapter 12. These campus visits should begin in November of your high school senior year.

The information that you have been able to gather in your college search efforts (although very beneficial) simply cannot give you a complete and accurate feel for the college's environment.

E-Z TIP
You must first visit each individual campus to get a true sense of what your life would be like attending that particular institution.

Arranging your finalists in order

After your campus visits (covered in Chapter 12) you will be able to arrange your colleges in order of preference based on the information you receive during the visit and the overall feel you get for each college. This will be vital to your final decision.

You should ideally list your top four choices, in order, based on your experiences and personal impressions of each individual school. These top four institutions should be the ones to which you believe you will be offered admission.

In addition to your top four schools, you should designate a 'long shot' selection. This long shot may be a school that has entrance requirements that slightly exceed your high school achievements. You should apply to this long shot school anyway; you never know. By following the guidelines in the next chapter, College Admissions Applications, as well as chapter 12, *College Campus Visits*, you may very well be able to sway the admissions officer into accepting your application.

You should also designate a "safety valve" school. This is an institution, such as a state-funded public college, to which you would surely be offered admission. These schools typically admit anyone who meets the minimum requirements. A safety valve is a good idea because, like the old saying goes, it is better to be safe than sorry.

Conclusion

The information that you have gathered as a result of research outlined in this chapter will go a long way in helping you determine your final college choice. Along with the knowledge you will collect during the college campus visits (covered in Chapter 12) and the evaluation and negotiating of the college's financial aid award letters (covered in Chapters 14 and 15), you will have the foundation for making your final college choice decision.

Chapter 7

College admissions applications

What you'll find in this chapter:

- Paper applications
- Downloadable applications
- Your application checklist
- Completing your application
- What to avoid on the application

The college admissions application process is the culmination of your efforts during the college search and selection procedure, which was covered in the last chapter. You have spent many hours researching which college(s) would be best suited for you, and now it is time to apply to each of your six top choices. We will call these institutions your finalist colleges.

> **HOT spot** Remember, a college will ultimately decide whether it likes you by reviewing one major item: your application for admission.

The college's admission officer is the person who reviews and evaluates your application. In fact, reading about prospective students, through their applications, is each college's admissions officer's number one job. He or she spends about fifteen minutes reading each individual application and any related documents that may have been requested by the college. During this fifteen minutes he or she will assign a score to your admission application and basically decide your future at that particular institution. It is vital that this reading material, your admission application, be as organized, complete, and accurate as possible. The real key to filling out and submitting your college admission application(s) is to actually know all the items the admissions officer is looking for and the prior arranging of all this necessary information into an effective admissions application packet. All of your high school achievements should be accurately portrayed in your admission application(s).

E-Z TIP
Your college application should be a detailed account of your four years of high school.

Some colleges' admission applications may be very complex and have many different sections. There are some areas of the application that may weigh much heavier than others do. Although most colleges choose not to talk about it, every college uses a scoring system to rank its applicants. The college's admission officer is the person who assigns each student his or her score. The college admissions officer assigns this score by taking every item included by the student in the application packet into consideration. It is important to remember that the most attractive students get the most generous financial aid offers.

HINT

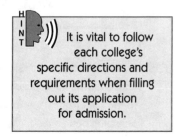

It is vital to follow each college's specific directions and requirements when filling out its application for admission.

Your college admissions application should do an effective job of accurately portraying your high school accomplishments. This will greatly increase your admission acceptance possibilities, as well as ensure you receive the most attractive financial aid award package if you are accepted. Knowing how to properly fill out the college application along with the necessary attached documents could literally make thousands of dollars worth of difference when it comes to funding a college education.

Making yourself attractive to the colleges will not only have a great bearing on your acceptance for admission, but also in determining your financial aid awards in the event you are accepted.

In this chapter we will show you specific ideas and strategies for preparing your college admission applications. This chapter goes into detail regarding the following:

- What items and information are needed and/or required and should be gathered and arranged prior to the filing of your college admission applications.
- When to make your college admission applications.
- How to make your admission applications effective and complete.

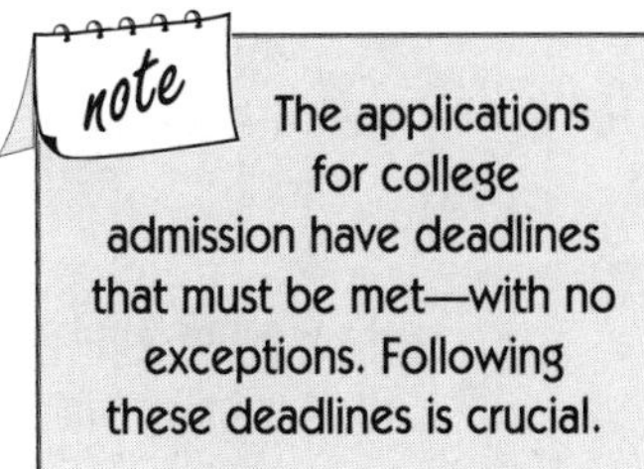

note
The applications for college admission have deadlines that must be met—with no exceptions. Following these deadlines is crucial.

When to apply

Ideally, the student will have completed a finalists' list of six possible colleges in August of the high school senior year (as outlined in the *Timeline*, Chapter 2, and also covered in Chapter 6).

The student should allow ample time (the *Timeline* in Chapter 2 provides one month) to gather all the information necessary to complete the college admission applications accurately and effectively. By gathering this information ahead of time, it will allow the student to have all the items necessary to make the admission applications at his/her fingertips.

> E-Z TIP: The actual college admission applications should be made in the first part of October in the student's high school senior year.

Although most college's deadlines for admission applications are usually in January or February (some are even in mid-December), the student who applies early definitely has an advantage. Most all students who apply wait to the last minute and their applications are commonly thrown in a pile with all of the other applicants. Putting your application in front of the admissions officers early will have many advantages and give these officers an opportunity to read through your application before they are hit with the large group of applications that will come in on the deadline date.

Methods of applying

There are two basic methods the student may use for applying to the colleges:

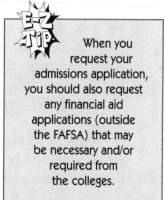

E-Z TIP: When you request your admissions application, you should also request any financial aid applications (outside the FAFSA) that may be necessary and/or required from the colleges.

1) A paper application, which may be obtained by writing, e-mailing, or calling the college's admissions office.

2) An application located and downloaded (printed) from the college's web-site. Most all colleges have a web-site and practically all of them have some sort of admissions application available on the site. Each college handles this a little differently. Some will suggest you print out an application and then mail it directly to the college's admission office, while others will allow you to apply electronically on-line.

HOT spot: It is important that you read and completely understand the college's directions for admission applications *before* applying.

Generally, the best practice is to apply to each college via paper application that may be obtained directly from the college's admissions office, or printed from the college's web-site. Because a paper application will take more time to submit it is important that the student be prepared and mail the application for admission in plenty of time to be received before the deadline of the college or university.

> E-Z Tip: Your acceptance will be based on your admission application. By completing a couple of practice applications you will have a much better feel when it comes to filing your application.

A paper application allows the student to make a copy and "practice" filling out trial applications before the actual application is completed and mailed to the college.

Items and information needed for completion of your college admission application(s)

The student should prepare ahead of time all the items and information necessary to effectively complete and submit the college admission applications. This may take a few weeks; in fact the Timeline in Chapter 2 allows a month for the gathering of this information.

All colleges are different and they have very different admission application requirements. By creating a "core" application file and including the below listed information into that file, you will have all the necessary items at your fingertips and be able to fill the admission application requirements for all of the colleges to which you are applying.

The information you should gather and include in your "core" application file:

____ Unofficial high school transcript

____ SAT and/or ACT test scores

____ Recommendation letters from:

  ____ Teachers, high school counselor

  ____ Community leaders

  ____ Business and professional people

  ____ Members of the clergy

____ A list of work experiences

____ 500-word essay on an experience that has special meaning to you (Some colleges may give the student a specific topic to write about instead)

____ A list of references who can comment on your skills and work experience

____ A list of volunteer or community activities in which you have participated

____ A list of positions held in school that show leadership and responsibility

____ Copies of documents and newspaper clippings verifying your awards, honors, and commendations

____ If you are applying for a program such as art, design, or music, you may have to include a list of your prior work, or you may be asked to audition on campus or submit an audio tape or similar sample of your work to effectively demonstrate your ability.

Most colleges' admission application requirements are found in a college directory. There are usually two or three good college directories available at your local library or you may wish to purchase one at your nearest bookstore. These directories are usually priced around $25, but are often a wise investment due to the fact that they may be used as a reference source for so many procedures in the college preparation and funding process.

The college admission "common application"

The *Common Application* is an eight-page form that tells the institution everything about the student applicant in a basic and simple format. The Common Application is now being accepted at more and more colleges and universities across the country. The Common Application was designed by the National Association of Secondary School Principals (NASSP) in order to make the college admission application process more convenient for the student and for the institutions.

If one or more of these schools will take the Common Application, you may be able to fill it out the first time and then make photocopies (make sure they are good, legible copies) and forward one to each of the other institutions that accept the Common Application. This will save you time in the long run and time is more important.

You may obtain a Common Application at your local high school guidance office or by writing the National Association of Secondary School Principals at: 1904 Association Drive, Reston, Virginia 22091.

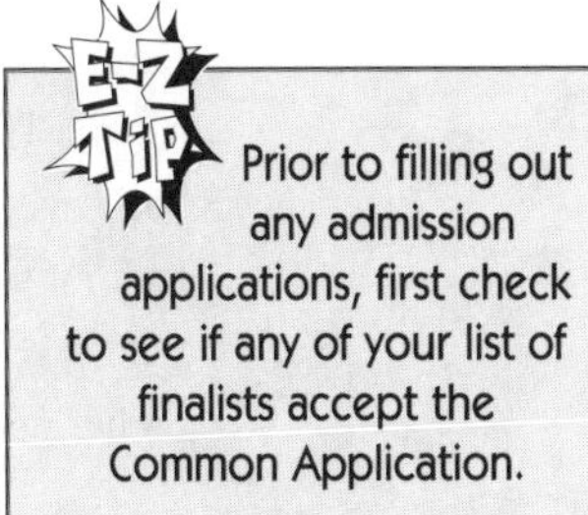

E-Z
TIP
Prior to filling out any admission applications, first check to see if any of your list of finalists accept the Common Application.

Fee for college admission applications

The admission application fee differs from college to college. The average college application fee is around $25; however, some colleges may run as high as $50 or $60. This application fee is usually non-refundable even if the student is denied an invitation for admission.

Questions and information found on your college admission application

The college admission application contains two basic categories of information:

1) Your high school courses, grades, test scores, and accomplishments. The answers to these questions have obviously already been determined by the time that you begin filling out your application. This section will ask for specifics regarding the following:

    a) Your high school transcript. The college's admission officer first looks at your transcript to determine which classes you have taken and how you have challenged yourself in high school. They then will look at your grades to see how well you have done with the courses you have selected. Colleges look for students who challenge themselves, rather than those who take a few of the "easier" courses and possibly receive higher grades from those classes.

    b) Your grade point average (GPA) and your class rank.

    c) Your test scores (PSAT, SAT I & II, and ACT).

note

This chapter on the College Admission Application is closely related to, and works hand in hand with, Chapter 4, *Preparing Your High School Transcript*. Chapter 4 goes into great detail regarding what the colleges are looking for in a student and how to prepare yourself for college while still in high school in order to increase the chances of your acceptance by a particular college or university.

2) Information (usually in the form of essays or recommendation letters) from you and other sources that provide an opportunity to fill in the blanks for the admissions officer. This information will give you a chance to offer a detailed account of who you are, what your personality is like, and an idea of your overall character to the person who is reviewing your application.

Specific items included in your admissions applications

Letters of recommendation

HINT

Letters of recommendation have much more influence on the admissions officer's decision than the student and parents often realize.

Letters of recommendation from teachers, high school counselors, community leaders, business people, professional people, and members of the clergy are the most underrated portion of the college admission application packet.

All colleges want at least a couple of recommendation letters. The two primary sources of these letters are your high school guidance counselor and one of your high school teachers. (When selecting a teacher to write your recommendation letter, be sure it is someone who knows you outside of your high school, and would be able to give an accurate account of your personality and overall character.)

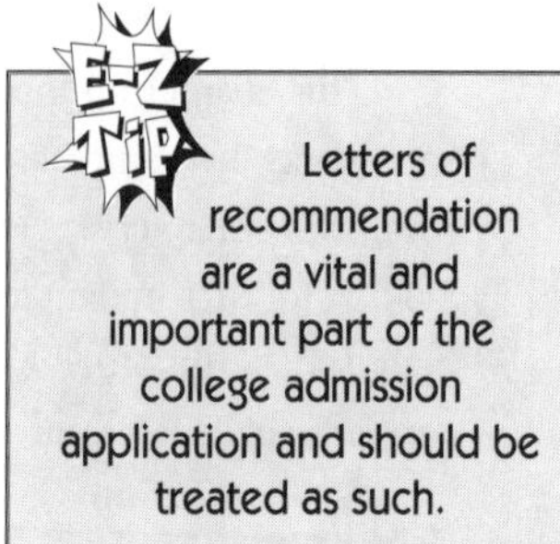

E-Z TIP
Letters of recommendation are a vital and important part of the college admission application and should be treated as such.

Due to the fact that the recommendation letter is such an important part of the college admission application packet, it is worth your time to get letters from all of the additional people (besides your high school counselor and teacher) that are listed above. When applying to six different institutions, there is a great possibility that you will need letters from all these sources, and by obtaining the recommendation letters ahead of time, you will save time and trouble when it comes to submitting your applications for admission. In addition, if a college gives you a choice of from whom you get a recommendation, you will be able to pick the best letter(s) for submission if you have a wide variety from which to choose.

HINT

Do not be afraid to meet with the person(s) writing the recommendation letter(s) *before* the letters are written.

Make sure the persons you choose to write your letters of recommendation know you as a person and will be able to effectively convey your accomplishments, goals, and overall character to the colleges. The content of your recommendation letters will often have a great deal of effect on your acceptance to the college and should be written by someone who can accurately describe your characteristics and accomplishments. Take some time and go over with them the items that you would like to be included, such as some of your accomplishments that might not show up elsewhere in your college admission application.

List your activities

Your list of high school activities is the next thing on your college application that is looked at by the admissions officer. He or she is not looking

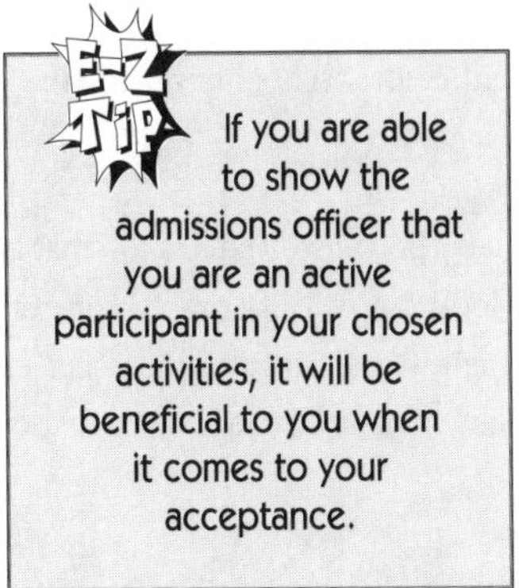

for quantity; they are looking for quality. They would like to see a student who actively participates in their selected activities.

A student who is in several different activities, but really is not active in any of them, is not what the college's admissions officer is looking for. These admissions officers want to find students who will contribute to their college's campus in more ways than just the classroom.

You should make a list of your activities, in order of interest to you, and include this list in your college admission application. Be sure to list everything you have done in school, community volunteer work, church, or any local organizations. In addition, you should always list your positions held with each particular activity to show the admissions officer that you are an active participant.

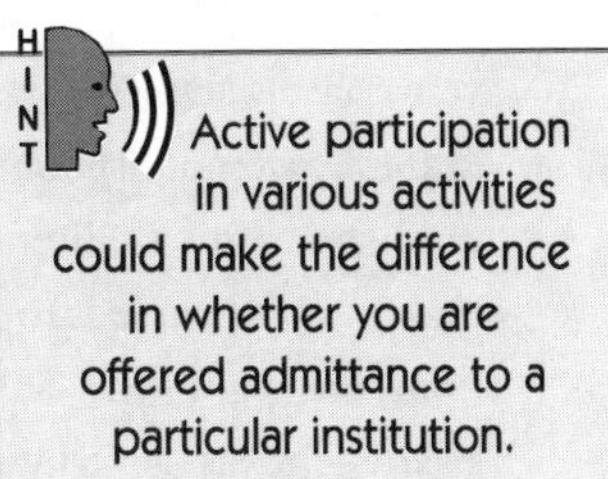

HINT
Active participation in various activities could make the difference in whether you are offered admittance to a particular institution.

Your activities will be important to the admissions officer who is reviewing your application. Make sure your college admissions applications contain a list of all your activities while in high school. Remember to highlight your positions held in each particular activity.

List of jobs, employment

The college's admissions officer also looks very closely at the work experiences you have collected during your high school years. You should make a list of the jobs that you held either after school or during the summer since you entered the ninth grade.

E-Z TIP

If you are able to show that you have been involved in a job that is closely related to your interests, this will be looked at very favorably. For example: If you take four years of theatre during high school, and are able to get a summer job in a related field, this would definitely demonstrate your true dedication to the occupation.

Work experience and the discipline that you obtain from it are very beneficial assets in the eyes of the college admissions officer.

List your awards

When listing your high school awards, you should start with the earliest award and move to the most recent. Even if you are a National Honor Society member and are tempted to list this as your first award, don't. It is far more important to list them in order, beginning with your first award. It is also important to list the awards which you have actually received. For example: Do not list your name being published in a directory simply because you agreed to buy a copy from the publisher. This is not an award—this is actually a marketing tool for the publisher, and the college's admissions officers know that. Be accurate in your list, and be honest. Remember that the admissions officers' number one job is reading admission applications. They are familiar with what are awards and what are not.

HOT spot

It is vital that you be truthful about your accomplishments and awards when completing your college admission applications.

Your college essay

The essay is one of the most important parts of your college admission application. The challenge you have in writing your essay(s) is to get the attention of the admissions officer who is reading it. You have a chance to express yourself as an individual and display for the college's admissions officer reasons he or she should offer you admittance, and you should surely take advantage of this opportunity.

The other parts we have previously covered in this chapter, which are contained in your admission application, tell more about what you have done while attending high school.

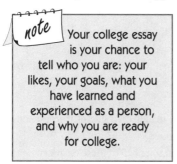

> note
> Your college essay is your chance to tell who you are: your likes, your goals, what you have learned and experienced as a person, and why you are ready for college.

The essay also gives you a chance to fill in the blanks in your admission application(s). In other words, it will allow you to fill the gaps between the statistics and facts of your admission application and the total number of your actual accomplishments and life-experiences during your high school years. The college essay should convey an honest, dynamic, self-motivated image of you.

The college admission essay gives you a chance to "stand out" among all of the other applicants. You should devote all the time necessary when writing your essay, simply because this essay could truly make the difference in deciding whether or not you are offered admittance.

> HOT spot
> Remember, the college is trying to determine what kind of a person you are and how well you are able to communicate your thoughts.

Colleges may request one essay (usually between 500 and 1,000 words), or they may request a combination of essays on related subjects.

note

Always give the college exactly what they request in their admission applications. For example: If the college asks for a 1,000 word essay on an experience that has had special meaning in your life, give them 1,000 words; not 700 or 1,500. It is very important that you are able to show the admissions officer that you are able to pay close attention to detail and follow directions effectively.

Whether the college requests only one essay or a combination of essays, you will find that the majority of these essays fall into one of the four following categories:

1) an essay about yourself

2) an essay about your extracurricular interests

3) an essay explaining why you would like to attend their particular institution

4) an essay showing the more imaginative side of your personality

Without question, the most common of all of these essays is the first one, "tell us about yourself." Due to the fact that this essay covers a wide range of possible topics, the student should be careful as to the content of this particular type of essay.

Simply giving a chronological list of events regarding the years of your life makes for boring reading and is quickly disregarded by most college admissions officers. It is much better to take a particular event in your life and focus on how the experience has made you into a stronger individual. Show the college's admission officer what you have learned in life and why you are a unique individual who would be an asset to his or her institution.

HOT spot When it comes to writing your essay, remember to accent the positive rather than dwell on the negative.

Prior to writing your essay(s) you should spend some time collecting and noting all of the valuable information regarding yourself. For example: Who you are, your accomplishments to date, your short-term goals, and your long-term goals. (You may also wish to refer to this information regarding yourself when preparing for your college campus visits and interviews, which are covered in detail in Chapter 12.)

Brainstorming

Next, you should put your writing skills to use and begin your essay by "brainstorming" in order to get ideas for your paper. Remember that you are simply arranging an outline and spelling, grammar, and the flow of the essay are not issues at this time. You should, in your brainstorming, include the following:

- Accomplishments that took you a great deal of effort to achieve. Include what the event was, how you approached and solved it, and what effect it had on you and your life.

- A list of personality traits that you value most about yourself. Also, make a list of how each of these traits has helped you in your life.

- Any major travels you may have taken. Make note of the impressions you had from the travels and how they have affected your life. Be specific and try to think of things that are not obvious, or experienced by most people who make the same visit.

- Make a list of all your activities during your four years of high school. Include:

    - awards

    - honors

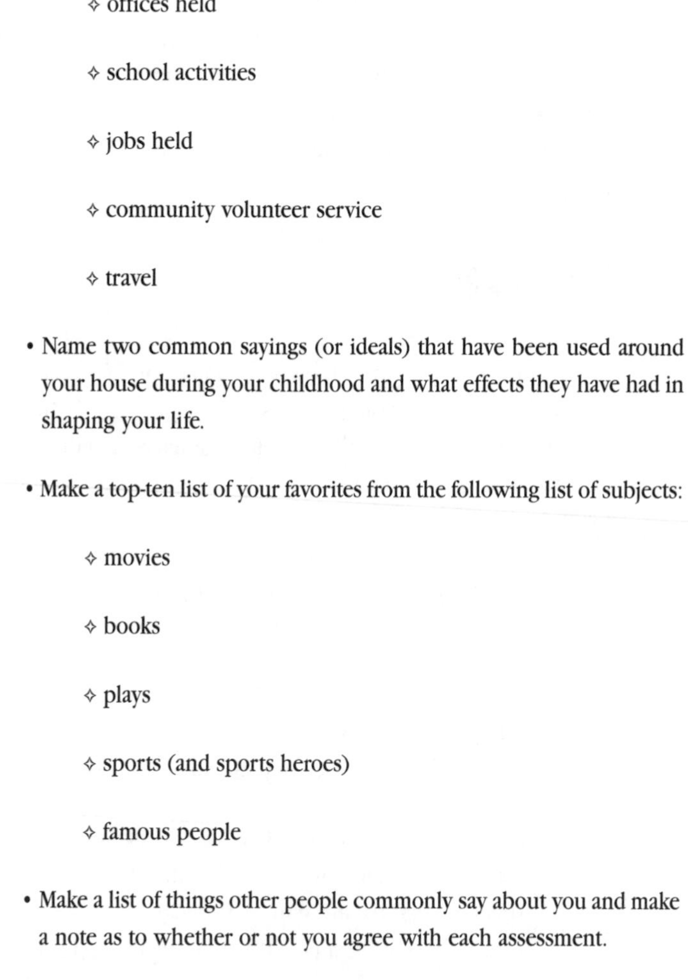

- ✧ offices held
- ✧ school activities
- ✧ jobs held
- ✧ community volunteer service
- ✧ travel

• Name two common sayings (or ideals) that have been used around your house during your childhood and what effects they have had in shaping your life.

• Make a top-ten list of your favorites from the following list of subjects:

- ✧ movies
- ✧ books
- ✧ plays
- ✧ sports (and sports heroes)
- ✧ famous people

• Make a list of things other people commonly say about you and make a note as to whether or not you agree with each assessment.

• Make a list of any people who have motivated you throughout your life and describe the way in which they motivated you.

First draft

You should now take the subject you decide on (or the particular subject assigned by the college) and begin making your first draft of your essay. There are basically two types of writers: those who preplan their work, and those who simply start writing and then re-write and re-arrange their essay until it flows naturally and makes logical sense. No one type of writing is better than the other; you should do what is natural to you, and what you feel comfortable with. It is important to let your ideas flow and your personality come out in your work.

HOT spot Remember, colleges are looking for the true thoughts, goals, and ideas of the applicant.

After your first draft is completed, it is time to read back through and decide which sections of your paper are working and which sections may need to be removed. You should be asking yourself, "What is the main idea I am trying to convey in this paper?" Your answer should only be one sentence. After you have arrived at your answer, go back and combine or re-arrange ideas in your work with this in mind.

E-Z TIP If there are several different ideas or events you wish to get across in your paper, it is important you determine the best way to link them together.

You should prioritize your ideas and give them a specific order of importance, instead of giving them all the same amount of consideration. It is important, however, to achieve a common connection of these ideas throughout your essay.

Here are a few hints that may help you in accurately evaluating your draft:

- Read your draft aloud. Your ear usually picks up problems that you would otherwise miss.

- Let your draft set for a few hours, or days, and come back to it with a fresh prospective.

- Ask your high school English teacher to review and make suggestions about your draft (and eventually your final copy) .

- Ask a parent or friend to review and offer their opinion about your draft.

Final draft

After you have had a chance to receive input from other people and review your work personally in your draft, now is the time to make appropriate changes. There are basically four ways to make changes in your draft in order to arrive at your final draft and the results you desire:

- add detail

- combine sentences to enable the ideas to flow more smoothly

- edit any phrases that may be repetitive

- re-arrange some of your original ideas

By using these techniques, you will be able to smooth off the rough edges of your draft and arrive at the final copy.

Below we have listed some other hints and ideas that may help you in your final draft preparation:

- Always run a spelling and grammar check on your essay.

- It is usually best to double-space your essay and follow all the writing procedures you have learned to make it easy to read.

- If a particular part (sentence or paragraph) of your essay bothers you, re-write it using two or three different options and see which one appeals to you the most.

- Ask your English teacher, and your parents (or friends) to proofread your final draft and give their honest opinion of your essay. Another person can often give a fresh view and possibly find things that you overlooked during your proofing.

- You should always type your essay.

- Remember to make your essay fit the specifications set forth by the college. Give them exactly what they ask for. If they want 1,000 words, it is vital that your essay be 1,000 words.

Remember, the college admissions officer is looking for three things about you when reading your essay:

1) how you write

2) how you think

3) information that they will not be able to find anywhere else in your admission application

You have the admissions officer's undivided attention when he/she is reading your essay. Make sure you take advantage of this time by writing an effective, attention-getting essay that will clearly portray your thoughts and character.

The essay is generally one of the biggest parts of the college admission application. Take advantage of this opportunity by writing an eye-catching paper that will stand out in the mind of the admissions officer who is reading it.

Important things NOT to do when completing your college admission application(s)

Below is a list of items that should be avoided at all cost when completing your college admission applications. A couple of these items probably seem obvious, while the others you may not be aware of. It is vital that you follow all of these tips when completing and submitting your admission applications:

- Do not write in longhand. Your application should be typewritten, and the included paperwork (such as your essay) should definitely be produced on a word processor or home computer. You should not make the admissions officer struggle to read your application. You definitely do not want them to simply give up on your application and move on to the next one because they were unable to make out your handwriting.

- Do not use whiteout. Remember that the admissions officer will spend fifteen minutes reviewing your application and it is vital that it be neat and well presented. Whiteout looks very unprofessional and the use of it should be avoided at all cost. If you use a typewriter make sure it is one with a correction ribbon. This is more appropriate than those ugly whiteout "blobs" all over the paper.

E-Z TIP
If you don't have access to a typewriter or computer and are forced to write your application, be sure to print (no longhand) using a pen, Make the work as legible as possible.

- Do not leave any of the questions on the application blank. If the admissions officer sees an unanswered question it shows them that you may be careless and that you actually pay very little attention to detail and/or directions. They may also think that you are purposefully avoiding the question because you have something to hide. If a question is marked optional, then you obviously have the option of leaving it blank. In all other circumstances make sure you double-check your admission application(s) to ensure all blanks are filled in and the application is complete. Do not give the admissions officer any reason to disqualify your application due to carelessness. It is best to first run a copy of the application and practice filling one out *before* you actually complete the final copy.

- Do not make the admissions officer search for the answers. In other words, do not use the phrase "see attached," and then have the readers refer to an attached page with the answer. If your answer takes more space than is provided on the application, you should begin the answer in the allotted space and then make a note to refer to an attached sheet for the remainder of the answer. In addition, if the application asks you for a test score (ACT and/or SAT) for example, the admissions officer knows that the score is located on your transcript; however, they want to see it on your application. Do not make them search for the requested information by putting "see transcript" on your admission application. Make it as easy for them to review your information as possible. It will pay great dividends when they determine your eligibility for acceptance into their institution.

- Never be a wise guy when filing out your admission applications. There is no room for fun and games. Your application should be serious, direct, complete, and to the point. Admissions officers are not looking for humor; they are looking for qualified students to fill their campuses. It is your job to show these admissions officers that you are one of those qualified students.

Chapter 8

Scholarship sources, types & availability

What you'll find in this chapter:

- Tips for locating scholarships
- Scholarship myths
- Types of scholarships
- Scholarship scams to avoid
- Your list of possible scholarships

HOT spot

Scholarships are one of the most attractive forms of financial aid for one very simple reason: the money is given to the student to help pay for the cost of his or her college education, and does not have to be paid back. Scholarship funds are a form of gift-aid, and as you will see in later chapters—the more gift-aid a student receives the less self-help aid (work-study and loans) will be required in order for the student to pay for his or her college education and degree.

Practically everyone has heard the term scholarship. There are literally thousands of scholarships available to students all across the country. These scholarships total literally billions of dollars in financial aid. However, locating scholarship funds is a very competitive and often time-consuming project. The student must be willing to spend time and

note

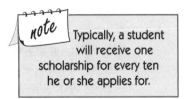

Typically, a student will receive one scholarship for every ten he or she applies for.

effort to locate and effectively apply for scholarships; however, this undertaking will most always pay off.

This chapter will go into great detail regarding the scholarships which may be available to you, and the proper way to locate them.

The next chapter, Chapter 9, *Application for Scholarships*, will guide you step by step through the scholarship application process and allow you to effectively apply for the scholarships that you were able to locate from the hints, tips, and ideas located in this chapter.

Statistics

There are over 300,000 different scholarships available nationwide. In the United States a total of over $28 billion worth of scholarship funds are available from the private sector alone annually. These scholarships are typically available in the following categories:

- academic achievement
- college major or career objective
- disabled individuals
- organizations and groups

The National Commission on Student Financial Assistance and the House Subcommittee on Post-secondary Education found that over one-third of all available funds goes unclaimed each year. One of the main reasons for this is the fact students simply do not locate the proper scholarship sources. Another reason for these unclaimed scholarship funds is that nearly 80% of all scholarship applications to the over 26,000 private foundations are either filled out incorrectly or are misdirected. Students often qualify for these awards; however, they either fail to locate them, or fail to apply for them effectively once they have located the scholarship source. Details on how to apply for scholarships efficiently is covered in the next chapter, Chapter 9.

Tips for locating scholarships

There are basically four rules of thumb to follow when searching for a scholarship source:

1) Realize that searching for scholarship funds is hard work, but will pay great dividends in the long run.

2) Be organized so that you may run effective searches and keep accurate records of your findings.

3) Do as many scholarship searches as possible from both local groups and organizations as well as the free web-site searches that are detailed later in this chapter.

4) Treat searching for scholarships like a job. In effect, locating scholarship sources is a job; however, an effective plan and a diligent effort will almost always produce gift-aid in the form of scholarships for college.

Generally, scholarships are reserved for students with special qualifications or interests, such as academics, athletic, or artistic talent; however, all scholarship sponsors have different criteria.

Scholarships are usually not need-based aid. In other words, the award is given mainly on the achievements of the applicants; however, financial need is taken into consideration on certain occasions.

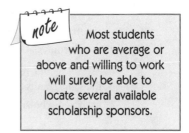

> **note** Most students who are average or above and willing to work will surely be able to locate several available scholarship sponsors.

Scholarship myths

There are several myths regarding scholarships. We have gathered a list of the most common, along with an explanation for each, as follows:

- I will never be able to obtain a scholarship due to the large amount of competition for the awards. It is important to remember that not all scholarships are for the class valedictorians. There are several scholarships available for students with particular interests and goals, for example: science, foreign language, leadership, public speaking, and the arts. Scholarships offer awards at many levels and the opportunities are very diverse.

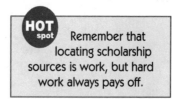

HOT spot Remember that locating scholarship sources is work, but hard work always pays off.

- Scholarships go only to the best students. Much like number one above, this is simply not true. In fact, scholarships are often awarded to students for study in a particular field. These awards may not require the student to be the highest academic achiever, but to simply meet the criteria, which is established by the scholarship sponsor. Again, this shows the importance of doing as much research as possible when locating scholarship sources.

note Scholarships are diverse and so are the qualifications you must meet in obtaining them.

- Paying for a scholarship search service is worth the money. False. It is not necessary to pay for a scholarship search. There are several "free" search sources (listed later in this chapter and also in the reference section of this guidebook, which is listed in Chapter 23) that yield the same results as a fee-based service. In general, a great many of the fee-based scholarship search services are typically scams.

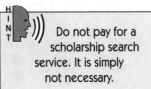

HOT spot If you have to pay in order to get a scholarship, it is probably a scam.

Details on how to avoid a scholarship search scam are covered in greater detail later in this chapter.

The myth that a student must pay for a scholarship search service is gradually dying due to the fact that people are becoming more and more familiar with the free resources that are available on the Internet and the World Wide Web.

HINT Do not pay for a scholarship search service. It is simply not necessary.

Many of the "free" scholarship search services are listed later in this chapter.

- If I apply for a loan, my chance of receiving a scholarship is not as good. Simply not true. First of all, these two sources (scholarships and loans) of financial aid are totally separate and independent of each other. It is important, however, that if a student has qualified for a loan and later receives a scholarship it is vital to see that the loan is reduced by the scholarship amount and another form of gift-aid (free money, such as a grant) is not affected by the scholarship.

Do not let the college replace free money with free money. Make sure the scholarship award that is received reduces the amount of the student's loan. This is covered in greater detail in Chapters 10 and 11.

- I am a top academic student and I will not have to search for scholarships—they will automatically be offered to me. Obviously the more you have to offer in academic talent, the better off you will be when it comes to scholarships. However, you still must search and apply for as many scholarships as possible. Again, scholarship searches are work, but usually prove to be very worthwhile.

Although you may have heard other myths concerning scholarships, these are the most common. They all show you basically one thing: Scholarships are available for practically any student who has the drive to do the necessary planning and work it takes to locate the scholarship sponsors. Most scholarships do not require a glamorous talent, or a top academic achiever; they require a plan, research, work, and dedication.

Scholarship facts

The facts listed below show the true depiction of the scholarship sponsored financial aid award system in the country today:

- 80% of the private sector does not require that the student show or prove financial need when awarding scholarships. This simply means that the private sector does not consider the family's income or assets when determining scholarship eligibility.

- 90% of the private sector is not looking to award scholarships to only the top academic achievers. Although good grades are always beneficial, students with average grades, and the desire and determination to learn, may receive a scholarship by falling into a certain category, such as:

  - Organizational affiliation.
  - Educational background.
  - Talent.
  - Ethnic origins.

- By making a scholarship search plan, and following that plan, the student should be able to find several different scholarship sponsors that offer awards based on their particular interests, background, or achievements.

Types of available scholarships

There are basically three different categories of scholarships. Each contains several different types of available scholarships. We have composed a list and explanation of each for you to review and familiarize yourself with:

- *Private scholarships*: These are basically groups and organizations which include, but are not limited to, the following:

  - ✧ Parent's place of employment—Your parent's employer or a labor union to which they belong may offer scholarships. There are a great number of companies and unions which have some type of scholarship money available for the students/children of their employees.

  - ✧ Religious organizations—Several churches, temples, and assorted other religious institutions offer scholarship funds for college. It is not always mandatory for the student to be of that particular religion or faith in order to receive the scholarship that is available.

  - ✧ Community organizations—Almost all communities have civic groups or similar organizations which offer college scholarships.

  - ✧ Corporations—Several of the large corporations in the country such as Chevron, Westinghouse, and Bank of America offer scholarship opportunities.

  - ✧ Ethnic or racial organizations—If you are a member of a particular ethnic or racial group, you may well be eligible for its scholarship programs.

- ✧ ROTC scholarships—These are offered by the United States Armed Forces and you will be required to serve as a reserve officer while in college in exchange for the financial aid award.

- Merit Scholarships: These are given by colleges to students who have demonstrated and achieved exceptional academic performance. There are currently more than 1,000 colleges in the country that offer these types of awards. The college will take the following criteria into consideration when determining the recipients of these awards:

  - ✧ class rank (standing) in high school
  - ✧ SAT and/or ACT scores
  - ✧ grade point average
  - ✧ financial need of the student.

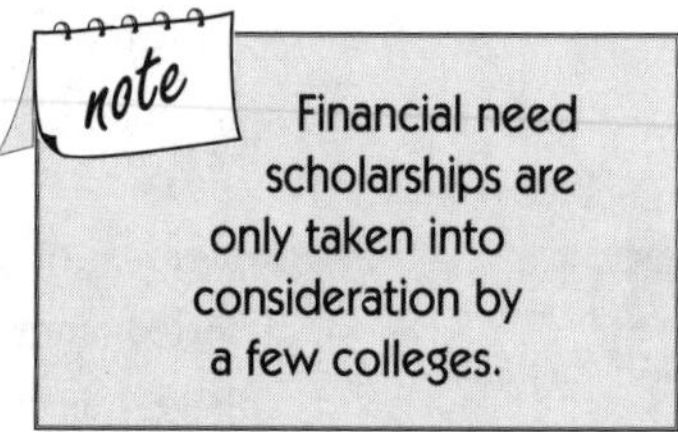

Financial need scholarships are only taken into consideration by a few colleges.

Check your list of the top six colleges you would like to attend, and inquire as to their availability of, and qualifications for, merit scholarships.

Remember that the more attractive you are to the college, the more lucrative financial aid package you will be offered. Details on how to make yourself and your accomplishments stand out for the colleges are covered in detail in Chapter 4, *Preparing Your High School Transcript*, Chapter 7, *College Admissions Applications*, and Chapter 12, *College Campus Visits*.

- University scholarships: These are available through the colleges or universities themselves, and include the following:

- ✧ Departmental scholarships—Are awarded to students who show specific aptitudes for an individual department or area of study at the college (mathematics, science, art, drama, music, or foreign language).

- ✧ Athletic scholarships—Are offered by most colleges and universities in order to attract the top athletes to their particular athletic programs. The major sports such as football, basketball, and baseball usually offer the most lucrative scholarships; however, scholarships are offered in a variety of other sports as well. These athletic scholarships are rarely based on academic performance.

- ✧ Fellowships—Money that is granted to certain students in order for them to pursue research projects at the college or university. Chemistry research is a common area for which scholarship funds may be awarded.

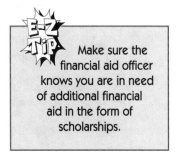

> E-Z TIP: Make sure the financial aid officer knows you are in need of additional financial aid in the form of scholarships.

When searching for scholarships that originate within the colleges themselves, it is critical that the institution's financial aid officer knows that you are actively looking for scholarship money. You should be sure to discuss this with the financial aid officer during your college campus visit, which is covered in Chapter 12. Also, during your college campus visit and interview with the financial aid officer, you should inquire whether the college awards its scholarships based on need, merit, or both.

These three basic categories clearly show that there are actually dozens of different types of scholarships available. The sponsors for these scholarships number in the thousands. The student must first formulate a plan in order to effectively search for the type of scholarships that will be suited to his/her achievements and goals.

Scholarships offered through a college or university are usually grouped into one of the following categories:

- Students who are interested in a particular field or area of study.
- Students who are members of underrepresented groups.
- Students who live in certain areas of the country.
- Students who demonstrate financial need.

Scholarship sources

Now that you are familiar with all the different categories and types of scholarships available, you should also begin to familiarize yourself with the sources where you may find these different types of scholarships. There are literally dozens of places to search for scholarships.

CAUTION
With today's technology, one of the most popular locations to begin your search is over the Internet and the World Wide Web.

Remember that we covered earlier in this chapter the need to be aware of the fee-based scholarship search services that are available today. The majority of these fee-based services are scams, and should be avoided at all cost.

There are a few reputable and legitimate scholarship search services available on the Internet today. Those services are free and have access to an extensive database, which enables them to often locate a number of scholarships, nationwide, for which the student may be eligible. These free scholarship search services will ask the student several detailed questions about their background, their goals, their achievements, and their family history. With this information, the search services will then provide a list of scholarships for which the student may apply, often including addresses and phone numbers that may be used for the application process. (The scholarship application process is covered in the next chapter, Chapter 9.)

Two of the best known "free" scholarship search services are:

1) Fast Web, which is located on-line at *www.fastweb.com*

2) Fast Aid, which is located at *www.fastaid.com/scholarships/steps.htm*

By using either one of these sources, the student can be confident that he/she will receive a list of available scholarships from several different sponsors which match a field of study, achievements and educational goals.

These scholarship search services also, commonly, continue to forward further available scholarship possibilities to the student via e-mail, even after the original search is completed.

In addition to these Internet-driven "free" scholarship searches, you may also conduct a local search for available scholarship funds in your community. You may wish to contact and/or search the following:

- clubs
- organizations
- agencies
- parent-teacher associations
- veterans groups
- professional organizations
- parent's employer and/or union

- corporations
- ethnic heritage groups
- religious affiliations/churches
- local Chamber of Commerce
- local libraries
- Yellow Pages (under foundations)
- American Legion Post
- local businesses (human relations department)
- high school guidance office

When contacting these different organizations, clubs, and businesses to inquire about the availability of a scholarship program, you should first call and then follow up your inquiry with a letter. Steps on applying for scholarships, including obtaining a copy of the application, criteria, and deadlines, are covered in the next chapter, Chapter 9.

Scholarship scams

Students and parents should be very careful when it comes to the Internet-driven scholarship search services. Although there are a few legitimate companies who conduct on-line scholarship searches (two of these legitimate companies have been listed previously in this chapter), there are several thousand students and families who have lost in excess of $100 million over the past year to fraudulent services. These scam operations will often imitate government agencies, grant-giving foundations, education lenders, and scholarship matching services. They often use official names like "national," "federal," "foundation," and "administration" in order to sound legitimate.

It is sometimes tough to determine which services are legitimate and which are scams. As a general rule, be wary of scholarships or scholarship search services that require an application fee, or a processing fee. Also, beware of services that guarantee success.

Typically, a scam will begin by the company requesting an up-front fee, which may range from $50 up to several hundred dollars. This fee is often advertised with a money-back guarantee. The company will then guarantee they will match the student with various sources of funding regardless of academic qualifications, family economic status, or other vital credentials. They often claim there are millions of dollars in unclaimed scholarship awards just waiting to be taken advantage of by students. They will then state that the student has guaranteed approval for the scholarship.

Only the scholarship sponsor itself can actually award the scholarship, not a scholarship search service. There is simply no way a scholarship search service can guarantee funds, which come from another source.

> HINT
>
> A good rule to live by when it comes to scholarship search companies: If it sounds too good to be true, it usually is.

All of these guarantees made by the scholarship search company mean simply one thing: there is really no guarantee at all. If a company makes all of these guarantees, and the service seems too good to be true, then it is most generally a scam.

These scholarship-scam companies may, in fact, run an on-line search for the student; however, it will simply be a list of possible scholarships. It is then the student"s responsibility to research and contact the scholarship sponsors. Claims by the bogus scholarship search service of guaranteed approval or guaranteed funds are completely false.

> HOT spot
>
> Remember, the scholarship sponsor is the only one that can award the scholarship.

Remember that the student has the ability to run an on-line scholarship search at no cost through one of the web-sites listed in this chapter. These web-sites, fastweb.com and fastaid.com, are both legitimate scholarship search services that will locate possible scholarship sponsors for the student at no charge. Their advertisers support these free scholarship search services.

E-Z TIP

In order to obtain a reliability report on the scholarship search company before signing up for their services, the student and parents should contact the Better Business Bureau in the city in which the firm is located.

To avoid being taken advantage of by one of the scholarship search scams it is important for the student and family to do their homework before they agree to sign with the company. These scam companies often prey on students and families who are rapidly approaching the deadline for school to start or students who have failed to apply for any other form of financial aid.

Compiling your list of scholarship sources and/or sponsors

While doing your research (from the many sources listed in this chapter) on the availability of scholarships for which you may apply, you should compile a list of your findings. This list will be used during the scholarship application procedure, which is covered in detail in the following chapter, Chapter 9. Be sure to include in your list the following information:

- name of scholarship sponsor
- mailing address
- E-mail address (if applicable)

- phone number
- contact name (if available)
- majors and/or area of study required for qualification of award
- value of award(s)
- application deadline
- items to be included in scholarship application packet
- rules of the scholarship application process
- number of points given for each specific portion of the application
- number of awards given each year
- description of the award
- any additional information regarding the award or the scholarship committee

After your list is completed, with hopefully dozens of scholarship possibilities, you are ready to move on to the information request and application process that is covered in the next chapter. It is important to keep accurate records when compiling your list of possible scholarship sources. An accurate list will save you time and trouble and make the entire scholarship application process much easier.

Chapter 9

Scholarship application process

What you'll find in this chapter:

- How to write a request letter
- How to complete the scholarship application
- Tracking the progress of your applications
- Tips & ideas to win that scholarship
- Do's & don'ts

There are several important steps involved in the scholarship application process. Writing to each scholarship sponsor to request information, completing your applications with all necessary materials and submitting each of them prior to their appropriate deadlines, along with tracking the progress of each scholarship application are all included in this meticulous process.

All of these steps are indispensable and must be followed closely in order to take full advantage of your efforts put forth during your scholarship search. Remember that in the previous chapter you learned how to locate the dozens of different scholarship sponsors for which you may qualify for an award. In this chapter we will show you how to take advantage of your effort by completing your scholarship applications effectively and in a timely manner. You will also learn the best method of tracking the progress of each scholarship application and how to make sure awarded funds are properly placed in your financial aid package.

The scholarship application process has three basic steps:

1) Writing to every organization that you have listed on your "possible scholarship award" sheet to request a list of the scholarship availability, rules, and deadlines.

2) Filling out the applications you receive properly, including your essay and any other requested material, and returning them to the scholarship sponsor prior to the deadline.

3) Following the progress of your scholarship applications.

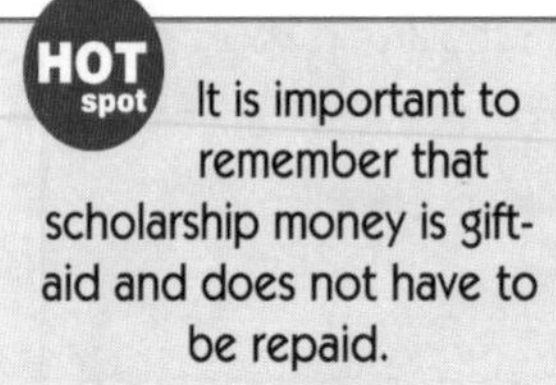

HOT
spot
It is important to remember that scholarship money is gift-aid and does not have to be repaid.

Many people often refer to scholarships as "free" money. Although scholarships are actually given to the student, it does require a great deal of work and dedication to locate, apply for, and obtain these funds.

In this chapter we will show you how to apply for scholarships effectively. It is most important to have a plan of action when applying for scholarships. You want to make effective use of your time. It's true that locating and applying for scholarship award money is work; however, making good use of your time will make the entire process much easier and much more profitable.

Information/application request letter

First, write to every organization that you listed on your possible scholarship award sheet. You should do this as soon as your list is completed, and as much in advance of their deadlines as possible.

Your scholarship application request letter should contain all of the following information:

- the organization's availability of scholarships
- a request for an application
- a request for a copy of the rules of eligibility—find out how many points are given for:
    - ✧ essay
    - ✧ need
    - ✧ leadership
    - ✧ work while in high school
    - ✧ involvement in school activities
    - ✧ volunteer work
- inquire as to the deadline for submitting applications
- inquire about other specific qualifications or help that may be required in the determination of the scholarship award recipients

HINT

Be sure to include with your request a self-addressed, stamped envelope—this will usually speed up the response time. In fact, some scholarship sponsors will not reply without a self-addressed, stamped envelope.

Your information and application request letters may be personalized on your home computer to each individual scholarship sponsor and/or organization. If you do not have a home computer, or access to one, you may make several photocopies of your original letter and then address each one individually; however, the little extra effort of a personalized letter may go a long ways in securing scholarship funds.

Use the first paragraph of the request letter to briefly introduce yourself and give a short history of the high school you are attending and what year you will be applying for admission to college. Using the second paragraph to request the necessary information (listed previously), mentioning the self-addressed, stamped envelope, and thanking them for their time, your letter will be direct, professional, and usually very effective.

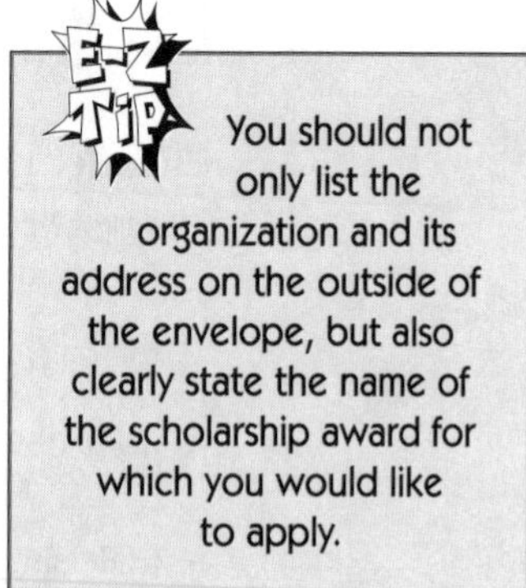

E-Z TIP
You should not only list the organization and its address on the outside of the envelope, but also clearly state the name of the scholarship award for which you would like to apply.

The scholarship application

Most scholarship applications are basically alike. They are usually one or two page forms that ask the following three basic questions:

1) Where do you go to high school?

2) What will your college major be?

3) Why do you think you should receive a scholarship?

Due to the similarity of the scholarship applications, you should first spend some time arranging all the information necessary to apply for scholarships into an effective application "package." If you arrange this information ahead of time and make a file for each item, you will save yourself countless hours down the road by having all of the possible required information at your fingertips. (The contents of an effective application package are listed later in this chapter.)

It is important to know and remember that the people who review the scholarship applications are looking for two particular things:

1) Something that makes you stand out over the other applicants. This is usually not an achievement, but the way that you personalize your application. The sponsors want to know about you as a person, not a name or number. You should clearly outline your ambitions, motivations, and what makes you different from the other applicants. Originality is a must. If you are able to portray the personal you to the sponsor, your chances of receiving an award will be greatly increased.

2) All the information exactly as they request it. Sounds simple. If they ask for a 500-word essay, give them a 500-word essay, not 400 or 1,000 words. Showing the sponsor that you pay attention to detail and are able to follow instructions closely will also go a long way towards you receiving a scholarship.

HOT spot
Remember, it is important to follow the rules and requests from the scholarship sponsor.

Your application should be neat, typewritten, complete, concise, and most of all, creative. You should mail your scholarship application at least one month before the sponsor's deadline.

E-Z TIP
Make sure all scholarship applications are submitted at least one month prior to the deadline date.

One of the main reasons so many students fail to receive scholarship money is they do not get the applications in by the deadline date.

You may find that some scholarship sponsors and organizations require that you join their particular organization before you may be considered for an award. If the organization pertains to your field of study, it would probably be good to join. This could also keep you informed regarding any new developments in the field.

Also, a few organizations require that you do your internship with them if awarded a scholarship. This is a decision the student will have to make; however, there are several advantages to take into consideration when making this decision. For example, if the award is large enough and the internship could evolve into a full-time position after graduation, this type of commitment may well be worth the student's time.

The essay

Most scholarship sponsors or organizations require an essay as a part of the scholarship application. The sponsor will either give you a topic to write on or allow you to pick a subject yourself.

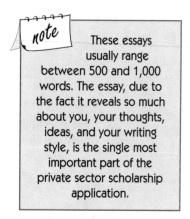

> note
>
> These essays usually range between 500 and 1,000 words. The essay, due to the fact it reveals so much about you, your thoughts, ideas, and your writing style, is the single most important part of the private sector scholarship application.

The scholarship sponsor is looking for information in your essay that will distinguish you from the rest of the applicants. In order to accomplish this, and make your application stand out, you may choose to write about several topics. Your personal goals, achievements, and experiences will give you an excellent place to start. You may wish to include any hardships, challenges, or unusual circumstances that you have faced. For example: Write on an important life experience you have been through and describe what you have learned from it.

Try not to simply make a list of your activities; those items are included in another part of the scholarship application and the scholarship sponsors do not want to read the same thing twice. Instead, take one particular activity and describe your level of achievement in that area. In addition, you may discuss the personal qualities that have been revealed during your accomplishment. Scholarship sponsors are interested in hearing about the student's achievements that have required motivation in order to complete.

You may also wish to discuss your interest in your intended area of study or college major. Informing the scholarship sponsor of your own personal feelings and thoughts regarding your selected area of study can surely go a long way in the securing of a scholarship.

Your essay should be photocopied (providing you are able to use the same one for each application and no sponsor has given you a specific subject to write about), making sure it is a good and clear copy, and attached to each individual scholarship application.

Additional information you must include

In addition to your essay, you should also be prepared to include any or all of the following information if requested by the sponsor: (Prior arranging of this information into a scholarship application package will usually save you time when the scholarship application process begins.)

- Your resume or curriculum vitae.
- Your unofficial high school transcript. Although you include an unofficial transcript with your original scholarship application, the scholarship sponsor must receive your official transcript copy before you may actually receive an award.
- SAT and ACT scores.
- Letters of recommendation from:

- ✧ teacher
- ✧ high school counselor
- ✧ friend
- ✧ employer (if applicable)
- ✧ community leaders
- ✧ business and professional people
- ✧ members of the clergy

HOT spot These recommendation letters should be from people who are able to comment on your skills, work experiences, and your overall character. It is important these recommendation letters paint an accurate picture of you, so they will stand out in the mind of the person reading your application.

- A list of all your awards and any newspaper articles you may have which would verify those awards.
- A list of positions held in high school that would demonstrate leadership and responsibility.
- A list of volunteer activities and any extra-curricular activities you were active in. Be sure to keep your high school activities and community activities separated.

It is very beneficial to gather and keep copies of all your awards and activities throughout high school to include in your application packet.

Some scholarship sponsors will be very detailed as to what should be included in your application package, while others will be much more open. It is important to include as much, or all, of the above listed information that is allowed by each sponsor.

E-Z TIP
The more the sponsor reads about you, and the more effectively you have arranged your scholarship application packet, the better your chances of receiving an award.

It may also be a good idea to include a high school photograph, either your class picture or a snapshot in your scholarship application packet. This will give your application more of a personal touch and may grab the attention of the person reading the application and increase your chances of receiving an award.

Arranging the necessary information to create an effective application package may take some time; however, this application package is actually the secret weapon that may win you thousands of dollars in scholarships.

Keep in mind that there are no real shortcuts. By devising a plan, and sticking to it, your time will be spent most effectively. Locating and applying for scholarships is hard work, and there are certainly no guarantees, but the rewards of your efforts can often be great.

> HINT
> Once your application package is assembled, you may simply tailor it to fit each specific scholarship application.

In order to increase your chances of receiving an award it is vital to arrange a powerful scholarship application package.

Tracking the progress of your scholarship application

By compiling a list of potential scholarships from the hints, tips, ideas, and strategies in the previous chapter, you will hopefully have located, and be able to apply for, several different sources of scholarship money. The different scholarship sponsors, along with different deadlines and requirements, can

make the scholarship application process very confusing. In order to prevent confusion, it is important to arrange a chart effectively tracking the progress of your scholarship applications.

Your chart should include the following:

- the name of the organization or sponsor
- the deadline for application submission
- the amount of the award(s)
- the number of awards given each year
- a contact name (if available)
- date request for application was mailed
- date scholarship application was mailed
- follow-up dates
- any other notes which are pertinent to the application

Arrange this information across the top of the page and then list the different scholarship sponsors, including their addresses and phone numbers, down the left margin to allow you to make a quick glance and evaluate your progress.

Scholarship sponsors are not required to inform you if your application has been denied, why it has been denied, or even if it was received in the first place. In addition, if you failed to include any required information in your application, your application will simply be removed from award contention. The scholarship sponsor will not notify you regarding your incomplete application; you will simply be disqualified.

E-Z TIP
You must make the effort to locate, apply, and track the progress of your applications for these awards—they will not come to you.

The scholarship sponsors receive literally thousands of applications and requests for applications each year. They will generally not make any special effort to help you with your scholarship application; they simply do not have the time. You must track the progress of your application yourself, from start to finish. Remember that this process takes work and dedication, but will often pay great dividends in the form of scholarship money for college. Scholarship money is available for all types of college students.

It is usually appropriate to contact the scholarship sponsor by phone if you have not heard anything within three months after submitting your application. Simply call them and ask about the "status" of your application. If there is a problem, and you catch it, perhaps you may be able to correct the situation and still be in contention for the award.

Remember that the scholarship sponsors will not notify you in the event of a problem with your application; however, they will usually tell you if you call and ask. In fact, by being courteous, you may be able to call and talk to the sponsors several times to check the status of your application. You are not being a nuisance; you are simply following the steps necessary to obtain the maximum amount of scholarship money for college.

If you, unfortunately, receive a letter stating that you did not make the final cut for a particular award, call the sponsor and find out why. Knowing the reason for your denial could be valuable information in the future; it may allow you to avoid making the same mistake with future scholarship applications.

Acceptance and placement of scholarship awards

HINT

Immediately after receiving notification that you have been awarded a scholarship, you should call and personally accept and thank the sponsor for the award. You should follow this phone call up with a short letter of acceptance, and thank you, addressed to the person whose name appears on the award notification letter.

When you receive a scholarship, make sure the amount of the award is deducted from the self-help aid (work-study and loans) portion of your financial aid package. Some institutions will attempt to take your scholarship money off your gift aid (grants and other discounts) instead of the self-help aid. At least, make sure both your self-help aid and gift aid are reduced equally by your scholarship. Please refer to Chapters 10 and 11 regarding more detailed information on the positioning of the financial aid package funds.

HOT spot It is vital to have your awarded money go towards money you would otherwise have to borrow or work for.

You should receive your awarded scholarship funds by July 15th. In the event you have still not received your award by the 15th of July, call and ask the person who signed the notification letter (the person you wrote the acceptance and thank you letter to) when you can expect to receive your award. The scholarship sponsor will usually be very receptive and eager to help any of their award recipients who have a question or concern.

Tips and ideas

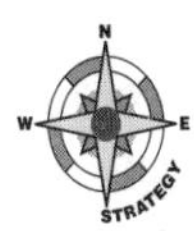

Although all scholarship applications are similar, every scholarship awarded is very different. Probably the best tip you could receive concerning the application process is to familiarize yourself with the organization offering the scholarship and tailor your application to fit. For instance:

- Knowing how the award was created, and by whom, is valuable information. This will give you a better understanding of the people who will be reviewing your scholarship application and possibly give you a related topic for your essay. Brushing up on the history of the scholarship sponsor, prior to your application, is a very good idea.

- Knowing what the organization does is important. This will allow you to submit an essay that may be in line with the company's product and/or business. You surely would not want to submit an essay with an inappropriate subject to a scholarship sponsor.

- Showing interest in the organization may be done by tailoring your application, and essay, accordingly.

- Compare yourself and your goals to those of past winners by obtaining a list of past recipients from the scholarship sponsor and contacting them.

- Contact the chairperson of the scholarship committee. Do not mail your application, or direct your correspondence, to a random person; addressing it directly to the chairperson is often a distinct advantage.

> **E-Z TIP** Receiving advice from past winners, and knowing how they presented themselves in order to receive the award, is a great advantage.

- If at all possible, schedule a personal interview with the scholarship committee, in addition to mailing your application. You should do further research regarding members of the scholarship committee and by using your findings you will be able to appeal to their interests during the interview. An interview will go much farther towards putting your name in front of the scholarship committee; in addition, it will also show your motivation and desire. When attending a scholarship interview you should remember the following:

  - ✧ Dress appropriately. Coat and tie for men and a blouse and skirt for women.

  - ✧ Always arrive at least 30 minutes early. Being rushed or disoriented could be costly.

  - ✧ Read the paper the week before the interview and brush up on current events. In addition, read up on a few back issues of *Time* and *Newsweek*. The scholarship committee will probably want to see if you have a general knowledge of world events.

Dos and don'ts

In addition to the above listed information here are a few other things you should know prior to applying for scholarships:

- Being active, and involved, in high school clubs, organizations, and activities will pay great dividends both to you as a person and to you when you begin searching for scholarships and/or financial aid.

- Good, solid grades along with high SAT and ACT scores will go a long way towards the securing of financial aid and in obtaining scholarships.

- Give each and every scholarship application all your effort, even if it appears to be a long shot. The extra effort may well be worth it.

- Be sure you select the most qualified people (high school counselor, teachers, etc.) to write your scholarship application recommendation letters. It should be someone who knows you outside of school also, if possible.

- Make sure you are always 100 percent honest on all of your applications regarding your accomplishments. If the sponsor reviewing your application has any question about your honesty, you have absolutely no chance of being awarded a scholarship.

HOT spot Do not shy away from scholarship opportunities because the essay request seems hard. Put a little more effort into it and you may well be at the top of the list.

Chapter 10

Financial aid

What you'll find in this chapter:

- Financial aid—common myths
- Gift aid and self-help aid
- Locating scholarship sources
- Additional sources of information

One of the biggest concerns everyone seems to have when it comes to preparing for college is financial aid. There are several facts and a few myths regarding financial aid, which will be covered in this chapter. The financial aid process is very complex and takes some time, effort, and dedication to understand.

Myths regarding financial aid

The following are common myths regarding college financial aid:

- Financial aid is only available to low-income families
- Financial aid is unavailable to families making more than $50,000 a year

- Financial aid is made up mostly of student loans and is basically just another way to borrow money

The most important factor in obtaining money for college is that the student and parents completely understand the financial aid process. This will allow the student to receive the highest quality education at the most affordable price. The financial aid process is very complicated, complex, and difficult; however, by following the hints, tips, and ideas outlined in this book, the aid process can be understood and completed successfully.

Financial aid supposedly goes to the students who need it the most. Financial aid goes to those who best understand how to find it and apply for it—those who understand how the system works.

The financial aid process has become increasingly more difficult over the years. There are now so many steps involved in the process most people really have no idea of where to start or what to do. Also, most people have the feeling they will miss a deadline, or not file a form correctly. This indecision can be very costly.

Applying for financial aid for a college education is probably one of the most complex and difficult financial experiences you will ever undertake. Again, learning the entire process is the real key to receiving the maximum amount of college financial aid. Students and families today should make a four-year financing and educational plan. This will allow the student to receive the all-important college degree and be able to pay for it at the same time.

DEFINITION

The term *financial aid* includes anything that makes up the difference between what the student and/or family pays and a college's published price. There are several different types of financial aid, and most of them require several different methods to obtain.

DEFINITION

Most types of financial aid programs are *need-based*. This means that the amount of aid received by the student depends on his/her particular financial situation. Most federal government sources of financial aid are need-based. The

other type of financial aid is called *merit-based*. These merit-based financial aid awards usually depend on the student's accomplishments. Academic, artistic, and athletic talent, along with high school grades, test scores, hobbies, and any other special talents the student may have, are the basis for the awarding of this particular type of financial aid.

Most financial aid requires the student be enrolled at least halftime at a college or university; however, some awards are restricted to full-time students. Financial aid may have many other restrictions as well. For example: Most federal aid programs are restricted to United States citizens, permanent residents, or eligible non-citizens. In addition, if you are a United States citizen, male, and are 18 years or older, you must be registered with the Selective Service in order to receive federal financial aid.

The two types of financial aid

The financial aid package is divided into two basic parts:

Gift-aid or gift money

A. *Gift money* is money that does not have to be paid back, and includes grants, scholarships, and fellowships.

a) **Grants**—these are funds that are awarded based on the applicant's demonstrated financial need.

1) *PELL Grants* are for undergraduates who have a demonstrated financial need. The maximum award is around $2,400; however, this can change. The Department of Education guarantees the college or university will receive enough money to pay their awarded PELL Grants, and they are transferable in the event the student decides to change schools. The student

automatically applies for a PELL Grant by completing the Free Application for Federal Student Aid—FAFSA. (Completion of the FAFSA is covered in detail in Chapter 11)

2) *Supplemental Educational Opportunity Grants (SEOG's)* are offered to undergraduates who have demonstrated financial need. These grants usually range from $200-$4,000 per year. Colleges and universities receive a set amount of money from the federal government, which they then distribute to students in the form of SEOG's. A student is likely to receive a SEOG if he or she has received a PELL grant. The student automatically applies for a SEOG by completing the Free Application for Federal Student Aid—FAFSA.

3) Several colleges and universities give institutional grants, also known as *tuition discounts*. Institutional grants are the single biggest form of gift aid, and will be included in the college's financial aid award letter to the student. These grants, or discounts, may be negotiated if necessary. This negotiation tactic is covered in detail in Chapter 15.

In addition to these grants, the federal government is now offering students the *HOPE Scholarship*, which is a tax credit for tuition fees paid. The government is also now making it possible for parents and grandparents to withdraw funds from their Individual Retirement Accounts, without penalty, to use for college expenses of a child or grandchild.

b) **Scholarships**—are a form of financial aid that are awarded based on the student's merit; although financial need is sometimes taken into consideration when determining a student's eligibility for a scholarship. Scholarships may be applied towards tuition, fees, and other required educational expenses. Most scholarships do not provide funds for living expenses. Scholarships are awarded in a number of different ways.

c) **Fellowships**—are awarded to graduate students based on the student's academic merit. Financial need is rarely taken into consideration in the awarding of a fellowship. Most fellowships provide funds for tuition, fees, and other required educational expenses as well as living expenses.

Certain forms of gift aid, such as ROTC scholarships and medical fellowships, require a few years of service in exchange for the financial aid that has been awarded. If a student does not repay the financial aid in the form of service, he or she must repay the money that was awarded.

Self-help aid; self-help money

B. *Self-help* is money that is either worked for or borrowed. Self-help includes work-study jobs and loans.

a) Federal work-study is available at practically every college or university in the country. Most of these jobs are campus-based, and are usually regulated by the college as to how many hours per week the student may work. The college also regulates the rate of pay the student receives. This program is subsidized by the federal government and may be used for the student's personal expenses.

b) The federal government often subsidizes educational loans, meaning the interest on these loans is deferred until the student graduates from college.

Sixty percent of college students borrow some amount of money to attend school. In 1997 the average borrower owed $17,000 upon completion of four years of college.

HOT spot You may have to borrow money to attend college, but remember there is plenty of money to be given away.

Although some of the student's aid package may be loans, if the "maze" is navigated correctly, the majority of the financial aid offered may be in the form of gift aid. Also, it should not be necessary to take a second mortgage on the family's home or buy special insurance policies to finance a college education.

- *The Perkins Loan* is a low-interest loan (generally around 5%) that is made available to low-income families. The student automatically applies for a Perkins loan by completing the Free Application for Federal Student Aid—FAFSA.

- *The Subsidized Stafford Loan* has an interest rate of around 8%, and is available to middle and upper-middle income families. The student automatically applies for a Stafford loan by completing the Free Application for Federal Student Aid—FAFSA.

E-Z TIP It is important to make sure that a loan is positioned in the "subsidized" category first, if possible. The interest will then be deferred until the student graduates and begins repaying the loan.

- *The Unsubsidized Stafford Loan* is not need-based, and the federal government does not defer the interest.

- The Federal PLUS Loan is designed for parents to borrow funds for all costs related to the student's education. Need is not considered for a PLUS loan, and payback usually begins immediately after the loan is taken.

Statistics pertaining to financial aid

In 1997, $40 billion came from various federal government programs to help students finance college. Most of the $40 billion goes to students who need it, because most of the government's aid programs are need-based. However, there are students whose families have six-figure incomes who receive financial aid in some form or another. This aid is also based on financial need; however, the government's formula that determines financial need also considers other factors besides income.

In addition to the government, every state also offers some financial aid to residents. The majority of state aid is need-based; however, some is also merit-based. Most state aid is only awarded to students who will attend a college or university in their home state. State aid, in most cases, must be applied for separately.

In 1997 another $9 billion came from the colleges themselves, usually in the form of tuition discounts, often called institutional grants. The tuition discount is a relatively new source of financial aid. Knowing which colleges offer these discounts is obviously very valuable information. The student and family may get an idea of which colleges offer tuition discounts by reviewing the college's financial aid history. If the college has a high percentage of students who are receiving financial aid and if the gift-aid ratio is high compared to the self-help aid, and also the cost of attendance, it is most likely the college is able to negotiate. Information on over 2,500 colleges may be obtained from the web-site located at *www.ecola.com/college*.

There are a few very wealthy colleges across the country that are able to admit any student they want without worrying about how much financial aid the student may need. These wealthy colleges have large enough private endowment funds to make up the difference for students if they want or need to. This information may also be researched during your college search.

Scholarship sources and information

Although most financial aid does come from the government, there are uncounted billions of dollars available, in the form of scholarships, from other sources that include:

- private foundations
- agencies
- corporations
- clubs
- banks
- fraternal and service organizations
- civic associations
- unions
- religious groups

note
There are thousands of scholarships offered from hundreds of different sources.

Most private scholarships are awarded based on student merit; however, some scholarships may be awarded after both the student's need and merit are taken into consideration.

HOT spot On average, a student who applies for ten scholarships will typically receive one.

It is well worth the time to do research regarding the availability of scholarships. The Internet, high school counseling offices, public libraries, and college financial aid offices are the best place to gather information about available scholarships.

Although there is countless information available over the Internet regarding scholarships, the majority of this information is free as the web-sites are actually sponsored by the advertisers. *www.fastweb.com* is an excellent "free" scholarship search resource.

For example: There is absolutely no reason for anyone to pay for the use of a computerized scholarship search service.

Additional information on locating scholarships is covered in Chapter 8.

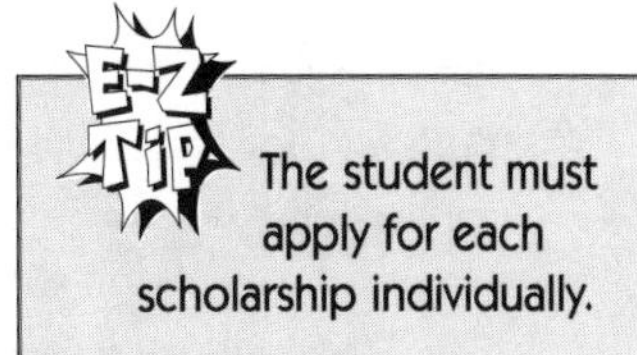

E-Z TIP
The student must apply for each scholarship individually.

In order to obtain financial aid through scholarships, the student must know how to apply for these awards in a timely and effective way. Please refer to Chapter 9, *Application for Scholarships*, for further information on the most effective method of applying for and receiving scholarships.

Additional sources of information

It is best to take the time to talk with both a high school guidance counselor and a college financial aid officer regarding the types of financial aid available. You may wish to briefly discuss your college plans, and the financial situation of your family. This will give the counselor or officer an idea of your situation and perhaps assist them in helping you locate additional financial aid sources.

Summary

Obviously, the best looking financial aid packages offer the student grants and free money, while less-attractive packages would offer jobs and loans. This ratio from grants and free money to work-study programs and loans depends, mainly, on how well the student's achievements have been portrayed to the college.

This again shows the importance of properly preparing and submitting the college admission application. Please refer to Chapter 7, *Application to Colleges*, for complete details on submitting your college admission application.

Most colleges typically follow the government's "need" formula to give away the federal money and then use their own endowment funds in order to build the college community they desire.

A very desirable student likely will have his entire need, and perhaps more, covered by grants and discounts—given the fact that he presents himself or herself to the college in the right way and at the right time. A failure to do this effectively may be disastrous when it comes to the financial aid package.

Locating and obtaining the gift-aid, or free money, first is the only way to do it. But actually knowing how to go after the free money is another story altogether. You must be able to work all aspects of the financial aid process. In order for the student to receive the highest quality education at the most affordable price each and every step along the way must be followed exactly and thoroughly. Sacrificing anything along the way will end up costing both the student and the family money and could also cost the student his or her quality of education.

HOT spot

Remember, the entire college selection, application, admission, and financial aid process is a highly sequential procedure.

note

Billions of dollars are given away each year to students who range from exceptionally bright and talented to average, yet eager to learn.

The money for college can be found in so many different places. It does, however, take planning, persistence, and dedication to achieve your financial aid goal. Committing to a four-year plan, and sticking to the system, will insure your share of the financial aid available each year.

One more key factor to remember—the amount of financial aid distributed each year will and does run out. There is an application "window" each year for financial aid. If you apply during this window, you will be assured your application is considered on its merits, and you won't lose money you deserve because a college has awarded all its cash.

HOT spot

Deadlines are the single most important factor in obtaining financial aid.

Additional important information

If you don't win financial aid your first year, you may not win any later. First-year aid winners always get priority at reapplication time. This means that the first year in college, your freshman year, is by far the most important. Your original applications for financial aid set the foundation for all your future benefits. Furthermore, financial aid is not automatically renewed. Financial aid is an annual event and must be re-applied for as such each year. This makes it so important to set a firm four-year plan, which will allow the student to receive financial aid throughout his or her college career.

Chapter 11

FAFSA & PROFILE

What you'll find in this chapter:

- Assistance for completing aid applications
- Gathering information for the FAFSA
- Receiving the Student Aid Report (SAR)
- Receive maximum aid with a trial FAFSA
- Avoiding mistakes on the CSS/Profile

The Free Application for Federal Student Aid, or the commonly used abbreviation—*FAFSA*, is what jumpstarts the entire financial aid process. The student's and family's assets and income are reported on the FAFSA and then submitted to the federal government. The government uses a formula called the Federal Methodology Need Analysis System, to then determine the amount of financial aid the student is eligible for. A copy of the FAFSA application may be obtained at most high school guidance offices or download one on-line at the government's financial aid web-site, *www.fafsa.ed.gov*.

The FAFSA is usually the only financial aid form needed by the colleges. However, there are a few selective colleges who also require a CSS/Financial Aid PROFILE form in addition to the FAFSA. The PROFILE is similar to the FAFSA, but the PROFILE asks for even more specific information in regards to certain assets of the student and family such as home equity, retirement accounts, and insurance policy values. You should only file a FAFSA with the government to begin with. If a college requires a CSS/PROFILE application, they will notify you.

The CSS/PROFILE application is covered in greater detail later in this chapter.

The information needed to file the FAFSA is similar to the information you would need to file federal income tax returns, purchase a new home, or a new car. However, the information required by the federal government for the FAFSA is much more detailed. The FAFSA is very involved and complicated, and must be completed both accurately and/or timely.

The FAFSA has a filing window. In other words, you may file your FAFSA between January 2nd and the end of February of your high school senior year, or by any deadline set forth by a particular college or university.

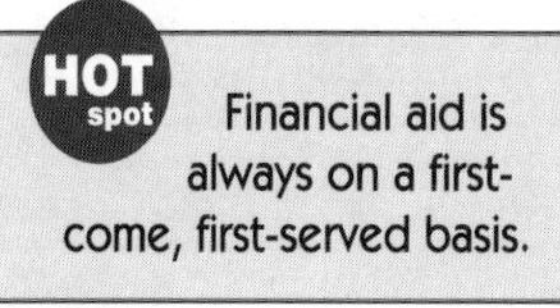

HOT spot
Financial aid is always on a first-come, first-served basis.

Filing your FAFSA on January 2nd, or as soon as possible thereafter, is a must for receiving the most attractive financial aid package. The federal government has only a limited amount of financial aid to distribute each year; financial aid does run out. By applying early you will assure yourself that your application is considered on merit, and you won't lose money you deserve because someone else filed before you.

After the government receives your information and processes your FAFSA, they will forward electronically their findings and determination in a report called the Institutional Student Information Report, or ISIR, to the colleges you have listed on the FAFSA application.

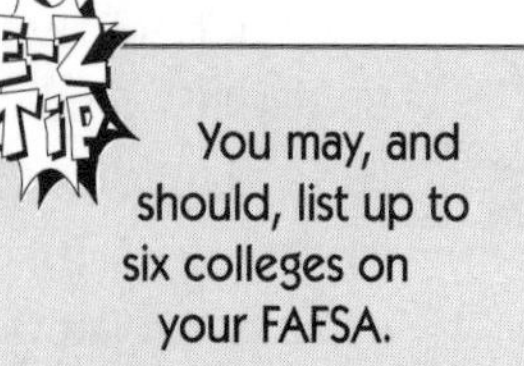

E-Z Tip
You may, and should, list up to six colleges on your FAFSA.

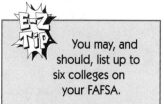

In addition, the government will also send you a report called the Student Aid Report, or SAR. The SAR

will give you the results of the FAFSA, including your Expected Family Contribution, or *EFC*. This EFC is the amount that you and your family are expected to pay each year towards the cost of your college education.

Often times, the EFC has actually very little to do with the amount the student and the family actually end up paying each year. By following specific guidelines and strategies outlined in this guidebook, the student and the family may actually pay less than indicated by the EFC.

After the colleges receive your ISIR, they will determine the amount of financial aid you are eligible for and notify you in the form of an award letter.

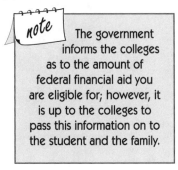

> note
>
> The government informs the colleges as to the amount of federal financial aid you are eligible for; however, it is up to the colleges to pass this information on to the student and the family.

When passing on the government's information, the colleges also include in the award letter any financial aid they are offering in the form of grants, work-study, and tuition discounts.

The colleges must distribute the government's financial aid as instructed, but they have the option of offering you a financial aid package, which is much more lucrative, based on your achievements and the manner in which they are portrayed to them. Chapter 4, High School Transcript, Chapter 7, Application to Colleges, and Chapter 12, College Campus Visits, discuss in detail how to make your accomplishments and achievements shine for the colleges in order to receive the maximum amount of financial aid.

This chapter covers the following topics regarding the filing of the FAFSA:

- Abbreviations, definitions, and terms you should be familiar with.
- Timelines and deadlines you should know in order to file the FAFSA effectively.

- Information and items that you will need to file the FAFSA.
- Procedures to follow when filing the FAFSA.
- Hints, tips, ideas, and strategies for filing the FAFSA more effectively.
- How to run a trial FAFSA prior to submitting your FAFSA to the government.
- How assets may be repositioned prior to your filing the FAFSA to enhance the amount of financial aid received by the student.
- Filing of the CSS/PROFILE application, if required by a particular college.
- Detailed information on the actual filing of the FAFSA step by step.
- Steps on how to track the progress of your FAFSA.
- After receiving the SAR, show you how to compare the figures contained in the SAR with what you expected and how to appeal or negotiate.
- How to correct and re-submit the Student Aid Report—SAR.
- How to ensure that all colleges you have included in your finalist list receive your SAR information, as well as federal tax forms, and W-2's.
- What to do if you are verified (audited).
- Information sources, web-sites, and phone numbers.

Abbreviations & definitions

Assets—the amount the family has in savings and investments. Any business or farm is also considered an asset when applying for financial aid. The net value of the family's home is only counted as an asset by some colleges who use the CSS/PROFILE application.

Available Income—the amount parents have available to help pay the student's annual college expenses.

Base Year—is the twelve-month period ending on December 31 proceeding the year in which the student will enroll in college. Example: students seeking aid for the 2000-2001 school .year will use 1999 as the base year.

College—any accredited post-secondary institution.

Cost of Education (Cost of Attendance)—is the total amount it will cost a student to attend college for one year, including tuition and fees; housing and food; books and supplies; travel costs directly related to attendance; child care expenses; and any costs related to the handicapped.

CSS/PROFILE—the application for financial aid used in addition to the FAFSA by a few select colleges. This application contains more detailed information concerning the family's assets, such as insurance policy values, retirement accounts, and equity in the family's primary home.

Dependent Student—a student claimed as a dependent member of the household for federal income tax purposes.

Discretionary Income—income that is available to a student or family after all financial obligations, including taxes, have been accounted for.

EFC—Expected Family Contribution—the amount the government expects you and your family to pay each year towards the cost of the student's education. This amount is determined by a congressionally mandated formula.

Enrollment—registered for at least half-time (six semester hours) for one term in a degree or certificate program.

FAFSA—Free Application for Federal Student Aid —the official application students must use to apply for federal aid. The FAFSA kick-starts the financial aid process.

Federal Methodology—a need-analysis formula approved by the United States Congress and used by the federal government to determine the amount each family should be expected to contribute towards college costs.

Financial Aid Award Letter—written notification to an applicant from a college that details how much and which specific types of financial aid are being offered if the student enrolls at that particular institution.

Financial Aid Package—the total amount of financial aid a student receives for a year of study.

Financial Aid Transcript—a record of any financial aid a student has received at a given institution.

Financial Need—the difference between what the student and family are expected to contribute to the education cost each year, and the total college cost for one year.

Gross Income—a family's or student's total income before any deductions.

Household Size—the total number of students who live with the parents who continually provide more than half of the student's annual support.

Institutional Methodology—a need-analysis formula used by the colleges, and the CSS/PROFILE financial aid application, to determine the student's eligibility for financial aid. This is a standard method of determining the student's or family's ability to pay for college. However, colleges must use the federal methodology in awarding any federal funds.

ISIR—Institutional Student Information Report—the report that is forwarded electronically by the government to the colleges that contains the results of your FAFSA, including your Expected Family Contribution (EFC).

SAR—Student Aid Report—an official document received from the government, which contains your Expected Family Contribution as determined by the government's federal methodology formula.

Unmet Need—when the combination of a student's financial aid package and the family contribution does not meet the costs of attending a particular college.

Verification—a process by which a financial aid office substantiates the data a financial aid applicant has reported on a financial aid application.

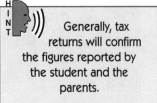

> HINT
>
> Generally, tax returns will confirm the figures reported by the student and the parents.

Timelines & deadlines for filing the FAFSA

High school senior year

December: Prepare and run a sample FAFSA by locating a financial aid calculator on-line which may be found at *www.finaid.org/calculators/*. This will give the student and the family an idea of what their Expected Family Contribution (EFC) will be and what may be anticipated in the way of financial aid.

The student and family may wish to try several different scenarios when running the trial FAFSA—experimenting with assets positioned differently to compare the student's eligibility for financial aid. There is a section later in this chapter that gives more detailed information on repositioning of assets that may be referred to when running the trial FAFSA. After experimenting with the trial FAFSA, the student and parents should make final preparations for filing of the actual FAFSA. Running a trial FAFSA is covered in greater detail later in this chapter.

The student and parents will be able to compare the figures and results from this FAFSA to the official copy when they receive the Student Aid Report from the government, usually four to six weeks after the FAFSA is submitted.

HINT
Be sure to keep a copy of the trial FAFSA.

January: Mail the original FAFSA on January 2nd (or as soon thereafter as possible), but before any particular college deadlines, and/or the end of February. Financial aid is always on a first-come first-served basis.

E-Z Tip: By filing the FAFSA on January 2nd the student will be sure to be first in line and will not lose financial aid because of failure to file promptly.

Estimated tax return information from the previous year may be used in order to file the FAFSA on January 2nd. The FAFSA may be corrected after receiving the SAR.

File your FAFSA on January 2nd.

You will usually receive the results from your FAFSA in four to six weeks. Re-file the FAFSA if more than eight weeks go by without a response.

February: After you receive the FAFSA answer (this form is called the Student Aid Report, or SAR) you will need to go back and review it, making changes or corrections where necessary. Use the base years Federal Tax Return form to correct and finalize the FAFSA. The SAR will have included an address where you may return the updated copy after you have reviewed, corrected, signed, and dated it.

The student and family should also send a copy of both the student's and the family's Federal Tax Return Form, along with attached W-2 forms, to each of the selected college's (listed on the FAFSA) financial aid office to be placed in the student's file.

E-Z TIP
Even though colleges will automatically get a copy of the SAR from the government, it is best to play it safe and send them a corrected copy directly.

March: The student and family will receive the corrected SAR form back from the government. The student should send a copy of this corrected SAR to each of the selected college's financial aid office to also be placed in the student's file.

Information and items you need to file FAFSA

You must be familiar with the following:

- Your parent's legal status.
- The history of your parent's retirement accounts.
- Your family's equity in its primary home.
- Your parent's job history.

Although you may not actually be asked to disclose all of this information on the FAFSA or other financial aid forms, it is best to have a general knowledge of this information before you begin applying for financial aid.

Items needed to file FAFSA:

- Student's and family's annual earned income.
- Student's and family's federal taxes paid for the year.
- Student's and family's federal Income Tax Returns. (You may use the previous year's return to estimate and then correct the SAR after filing the current [base] year's return.)
- All W-2 forms and any other records of money earned by both the student and the family.
- Copies of the student's and family's last payroll stubs.
- Untaxed income received:

  a) Social Security benefits

  b) Child support

  c) Welfare

  d) Tax-deferred income programs (401K, etc.)

  e) AFDC

  f) ADC

  g) Housing allowances
- All checking and savings account records and balances.
- All investments, investment balances, and interest information including stocks, bonds, and any other investments of the student and the family.

- Values of any business and/or farm owned by the family and the records pertaining to each.

- The student's driver license number and Social Security number.

Procedures to follow when filing the FAFSA

- File as soon after January 1st as possible. Financial aid is always on a first-come, first-serve basis.

- Mail your FAFSA by regular first-class mail. Special delivery will only slow down the process. Send the corrected FAFSA (in the form of an SAR, if applicable) by regular first-class mail also.

- The FAFSA may also be filed electronically at the government's website, which is located at www.fafsa.ed.gov. This site has easy-to-follow instructions and the student's FAFSA will be filed instantly. The student and parents will receive a signature page in the mail that must be signed and returned before the FAFSA is processed.

note
The student does not have to be accepted by a college or university before filing the FAFSA.

Sign and return the FAFSA signature page immediately.

- Two effective methods of tracking the progress of your FAFSA:

  1) Call your college's financial aid office and check if they have received the results of your FAFSA approximately four weeks after it was filed. At the same time you may inform the college's financial aid counselor that you will be sending him or her a copy of your corrected FAFSA (if applicable), along with the parent's and student's federal tax return forms, and W-2 forms for both.

2) Call FAFSA directly at (319) 337-5665.

- SAR—Student Aid Report. The SAR is the end result of submitting the FAFSA. You should generally receive the SAR within 4 to 6 weeks after filing your FAFSA. The main purpose of the SAR is to notify the student and family what their Expected Family Contribution (EFC) is going to be. The EFC is located in the upper right-hand corner of the SAR directly under the processing date.

You always want the lowest possible EFC. The lower the EFC, the less the government expects the student and the family to contribute towards the cost of education.

E-Z TIP

If there is a change in financial condition of the student or the family (loss of job, etc.) notify each financial aid office of every college you have selected and listed on the FAFSA immediately. This is covered in greater detail in Chapter 15, *Negotiating College Award Letters*.

Definition:

The cost of college minus your EFC is defined as your *demonstrated need.*

The Student Aid Report (SAR)

Part I — Is a copy of all the information that you originally submitted.

Part II — Is the correction page where you may make revisions and update the estimated information you used when originally filing. You should return only Part II to the specified "Department of Education Processor" by using the return envelope, and/or address, that is provided for you.

Be sure to make copies of corrections in Part II and send them to the financial aid office of each of your selected colleges, keeping a copy for your files.

Important items to double-check on the SAR:

- The student's social security number.
- Make sure the tax return information for the base application year is reflected correctly on the FAFSA.
- Make sure all the colleges that you have chosen to receive your SAR are listed.
- Correct the SAR promptly and return it to the "Department of Education Processor."

College Award Letter

After the colleges receive all the corrected and updated information contained in your SAR from the government, they will then send the student what is called an "Award Letter." This award letter will contain the institution's financial aid proposal, as well as any federal financial aid that will be awarded. The award letter will have monies that are available to the student through both the government and the colleges themselves. This award letter will constitute the student's entire financial aid package.

Hints, tips, ideas, and strategies for filing the FAFSA

File the FAFSA carefully and precisely. Several of the questions may actually seem too easy and may be very misleading. Do not take anything for granted when filing the FAFSA and make sure every blank is filled in.

- Use numbers or a zero to respond to all questions. Do not leave any questions or spaces blank unless that option is clearly stated on the application.

- Do not enclose, staple or attach any documents to the FAFSA.

- Use numbers to reflect dates. Example: 11-01-98

- All numbers should be rounded off to the nearest dollar.

- The term "school," when used in the FAFSA, refers to post-secondary institution (college or university).

- Always make and keep two copies of all documents and correspondences. The parents should keep a set of copies and the student should also have separate copies.

- The FAFSA should be filed as soon after January 1st as possible. Financial aid is first-come first-served and must be applied for as such.

- The student's and parent's federal income tax return is the main source of information used in filing the FAFSA. Due to the fact tax returns are usually not completed by January 2nd, it is acceptable, in fact encouraged, to use estimates from the previous year's returns and make corrections in February when the Student Aid Report is received.

- The base year is the 12 month period ending on December 31 preceding the year in which the student will enroll in college. Example: Students seeking aid for the 2000-2001 school year will use 1999 as the base year.

- If the natural parents are separated or divorced, the custodial parent (the parent with whom the student lived and received the majority of his or her support from during the past 12 months) fills out the FAFSA. In most cases the financial information from the non-custodial parent is never used when applying for financial aid.

A list of items that are commonly excluded from the FAFSA:

- tuition prepayment plans
- the value (equity) of the parent's home
- tax deferred retirement accounts
- cash value of life insurance policies

The number of students in the family who will be attending college simultaneously must be reported accurately on the FAFSA.

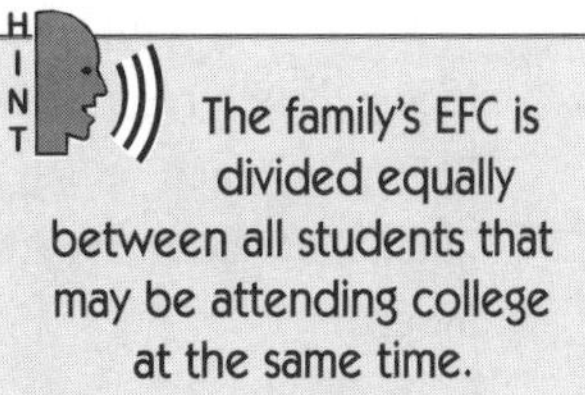

HINT
The family's EFC is divided equally between all students that may be attending college at the same time.

Running a trial FAFSA

You may find a financial aid calculator on-line at *www.finaid.org/calculators/*. This will allow you to run a trial FAFSA, by plugging in the family's financial information, and receive a projected Expected Family Contribution—EFC. By running a trial FAFSA and experimenting with several different scenarios from the student's and family's income, assets, investments, farm, and business, both the student and the family will have an idea of what they may expect in the form of financial aid. You may use the information, which is located next in this chapter—under "repositioning assets"—to help you in running your trial FAFSA.Print and keep a copy of the trial FAFSA for a reference guide later in the process.

It is important to run a trial FAFSA for several reasons. You will be able to experiment and find the perfect scenario for both the student and the family. In addition, the student and parents will have a reference guide that may be referred to when the Student Aid Report is received from the government.

Repositioning assets

When applying for financial aid, both the student and family will be asked questions very similar to those asked when buying a car or a home. The information contained in the FAFSA is very much like that of an income tax return. However, the FAFSA is much more complicated, much more detailed and has no room for error.

> **HOT spot** The key is to know what should be included and what may be omitted in order for the student and the family to receive the most lucrative financial aid package.

The government uses a formula for calculating the student's and family's contribution. This contribution is known as the Expected Family Contribution, or its commonly used abbreviation—EFC.

Savings account assets

The government's formula takes only about 5% of the parent's savings account assets into consideration when figuring the EFC, but takes over 35% of the student's. For that reason, families may want all savings account funds to be used for college to be in the name of the parents and not the student. Simply by repositioning these monies, it could lower the family's EFC and consequentially make thousands of dollars worth of difference in what the student and family will actually pay towards the cost of the student's college education.

Shifting saving account assets from the student's to the parent's name is exactly the opposite of what you would do to save taxes. Children's interest income is usually taxed at a lower rate. In fact, for children under the age of 14, the first $600 of interest earned each year is tax-free. Therefore, the family must carefully consider where they should position the money in savings accounts. They must determine which is the best scenario for their particular situation. The family may wish to consult with their tax accountant for further advice on the positioning of savings account assets.

Tax-deferred retirement funds

The government only considers the parent's assets that are invested in an IRA or similar tax-deferred retirement fund in the calendar year before applying for financial aid. All retirement savings accumulated before January of the student's high school junior year are ignored by the government's formulas.

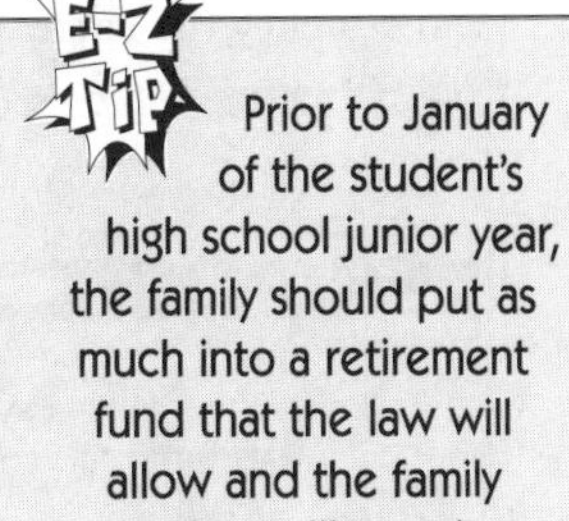

Prior to January of the student's high school junior year, the family should put as much into a retirement fund that the law will allow and the family budget will permit.

When to sell investments?

If you plan to sell any type of investments to help raise money for a college education, it is very important that you do so early in the student's high school junior year. Any capital gains that are earned the base year before you apply for financial aid, (from January of the eleventh grade to December of the twelfth grade) will be counted by the government as income when it comes to determining the student's financial aid need. To prevent this, you must sell investments before January of the student's high school junior year.

Medical and dental expenses

Medical and dental expenses that are not covered by insurance are usually deducted from your income by most of the colleges who require the CSS/PROFILE supplemental financial aid form. It would generally benefit the parents to pay all medical bills possible by the end of the student's base application year (December of the student's high school senior year).

Home equity

This is an asset the government's formula does not take into consideration when it comes to calculating financial aid need. In fact, the more money the family is able to put towards home equity, the less out-of-pocket money will be required to pay for college.

CSS/PROFILE Application

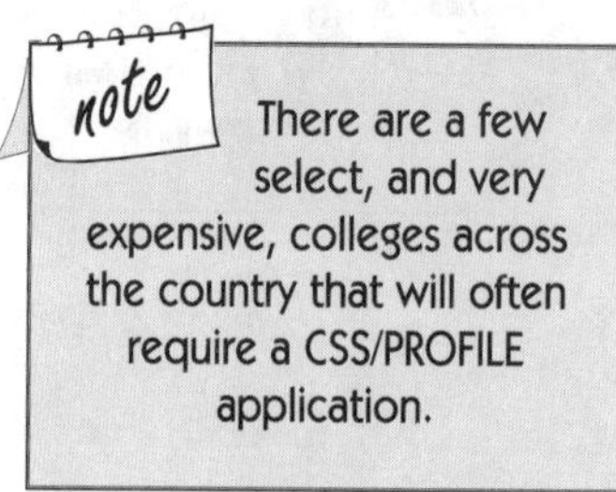

note
There are a few select, and very expensive, colleges across the country that will often require a CSS/PROFILE application.

The PROFILE application duplicates all the questions on the FAFSA, but goes into greater detail regarding specific items such as home equity, insurance policies, and retirement accounts when calculating financial aid need. The PROFILE application uses the "Institutional Methodology System" to calculate financial aid need, and the FAFSA uses the "Federal Methodology System."

If a college you have selected requires a CSS/PROFILE application, that particular college will contact you and request a PROFILE.

The CSS/PROFILE is not a free application like the FAFSA—it will usually cost around $20. However, the PROFILE application is well worth it. You cannot afford to ignore a request for a PROFILE application. It will be time and money well spent.

> note
>
> Typically, any school requesting a PROFILE usually has an abundance of money to give away.

If a college or university requires a CSS/PROFILE, the student must first send in a PROFILE registration form and request an application. These registration forms are available at most high school guidance offices, or you may find one on-line at the College Board's web-site, located at *www.collegeboard.com/finaid/fastud/html/proform001.html.*

The *PROFILE registration* is a one-page form that will ask basic demographic information about the student's family and also ask for a listing of all the colleges that have requested a PROFILE financial aid form.

Do not list any colleges on the PROFILE other than the ones who have actually requested the CSS/PROFILE application.

The student then mails the registration form, along with the required payment, to the College Scholarship Service, whose address will be listed on the registration. Overnight service may be requested if the financial aid deadline is approaching fast.

In a few weeks (unless overnight service has been requested) the student will receive the CSS/PROFILE financial aid application form. The PROFILE application packet will contain the following:

- All questions necessary to estimate your family contribution based on the federal formula plus the specific questions the colleges want answered.
- Codes to tell you which colleges want which additional information.
- Cover letter with information about deadlines and any special requirements from the colleges requesting the information.
- Any supplemental forms required by the colleges, such as a business/farm supplement form.

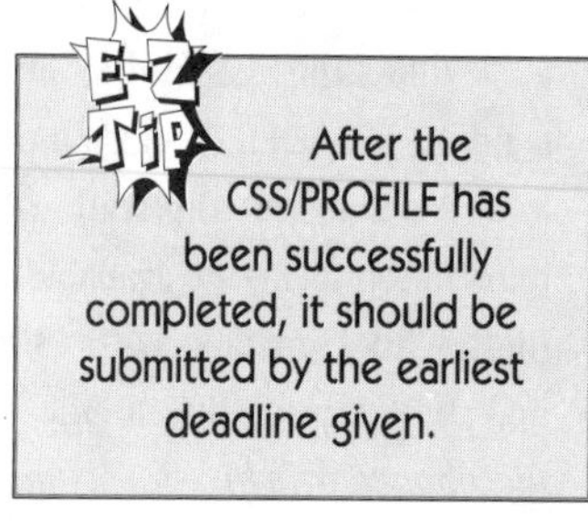

E-Z Tip
After the CSS/PROFILE has been successfully completed, it should be submitted by the earliest deadline given.

Between two and four weeks after your submission you should receive an acknowledgment and a report that will contain your estimated federal Expected Family Contribution (from the FAFSA) and a second family contribution calculated from the additional data you have provided. This is referred to as the "Institutional Methodology." Colleges that require the CSS/PROFILE use this methodology when they award their own funds in conjunction with federal aid.

Be sure to list only the colleges that have requested the PROFILE on the PROFILE application. On the FAFSA the student should list all of his or her final six college choices.

A PROFILE application does not take the place of the FAFSA. You must always file the FAFSA first, even if the college requests a CSS/PROFILE. The PROFILE application is always in addition to the FAFSA.

Even though the CSS/PROFILE financial aid application is very detailed and takes time to apply for and file, it will prove to be well worth the time. Any college or university who requires the CSS/PROFILE usually has an abundance of financial aid to distribute. Make sure the PROFILE is filed accurately and promptly to ensure you will receive all the financial aid the institution has available for you.

Detailed line-by-line instructions on filing the FAFSA

The FAFSA contains several questions that may be confusing and misleading. Below is a list of common mistakes made on the FAFSA application (line by line) and hints on ways to avoid making an incorrect entry on the FAFSA.

The student and family will be able to check and make any necessary adjustments, using updated tax information, to the original FAFSA application after they have received the results of the FAFSA from the government in the form of a Student Aid Report (SAR).

> **HOT spot** Estimates are acceptable, in fact encouraged, on the FAFSA application.

Common FAFSA mistakes, and questions that may be misleading, along with ways to avoid them:

- Questions 8 and 9—when asking for the Social Security Number and Date of Birth it is referring to that of the student.

- Question 16—it is asking for the marital status of the student.

- Questions 34 and 35—the student should check "yes" to both in regards to his or her interest in obtaining student loans and work-study financial aid. Even though this form of financial aid may not be necessary, do not rule out or decline any type of financial aid at this point.

- Questions 38 and 39—refers to the status and type of income tax return form that is or will be filed by the student.
- Questions 40 through 52—are pertaining to the income and assets of the student.
- Question 49—is regarding the student's current cash, savings, and checking account balances and is an area where assets may be re-positioned to provide for more financial aid.
- Questions 53 through 57—determine if the student is dependent on his/her parents. If "no" is answered in all locations (which is usually the case for a high school senior attending college for the first time), the student is dependent and the parent's information will need to be included in the application.
- Question 58—refers to children and/or dependents of the student.
- Questions 59 and 60—pertain to the student and should only be answered if the student answered "yes" to any of the questions 53 through 57.
- Questions 61 through 82—are questions regarding the parent's assets and income. The parents must complete these, or the custodial parent in the event the natural parents are divorced.
- Question 72—is regarding the parent's current cash, savings, and checking account balances and is an area where assets may be re-positioned to provide for more financial aid.
- Question 78—asks how many people in the parent's household will be college students. Be sure to include the applying student in that total (the answer will always be at least one).
- Questions 83 through 94—determine which colleges receive the student's financial aid information from the government. Be very

precise when entering this information—include complete college name, street address, city, and state. Checking "on-campus" housing could possibly make the student eligible for additional financial aid.

✧ Questions 95 and 96—be sure to double check the entire form and then sign and date the form.

Make two copies, and mail (by regular first-class mail) the original completed FAFSA on January 2nd, or as soon thereafter as possible. Financial aid is always first-come first-served. Being first in line is a priority.

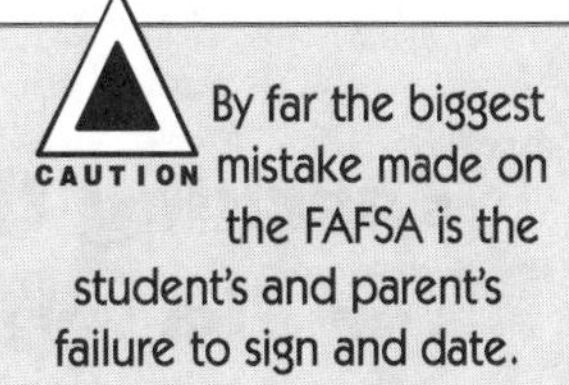

CAUTION
By far the biggest mistake made on the FAFSA is the student's and parent's failure to sign and date.

note

In the event you choose to file the FAFSA electronically, through the government's web-site located at *www.fafsa.ed.gov*, be sure to print a copy for your records. In addition, make sure you receive, sign, and promptly return the "signature page"—which will be sent to you by the government.

Tracking the progress of the FAFSA

The processing of the FAFSA usually takes between four and six weeks. To check the progress of the FAFSA during this time, the student may call the FAFSA processing center directly at (319) 337-5665. In addition, the student may call the colleges' financial aid offices and ask if they have received the results of your FAFSA.

HOT spot

Tracking of the FAFSA may begin four weeks after it's original submission.

If you call the financial aid offices to check the status of the FAFSA, you should also inform the college's financial aid counselor that you will be sending him or her a corrected copy of your FAFSA (if applicable). In addition you will forward a copy of the parent's and student's federal tax return forms, and all W-2 forms.

If eight weeks have gone by and you haven't received the Student Aid Report (SAR) from the government, you should re-file your FAFSA. It is important to keep the dated copies of the original FAFSA. These could prove beneficial if re-filing is necessary.

Checking the Student Aid Report for discrepancies

The answer to the FAFSA will come in the form of a Student Aid Report, or SAR. This report will contain two parts:

1) A copy of all the original information you and your family provided.

2) A place to make any necessary changes, or corrections and return the updated FAFSA to the processing center.

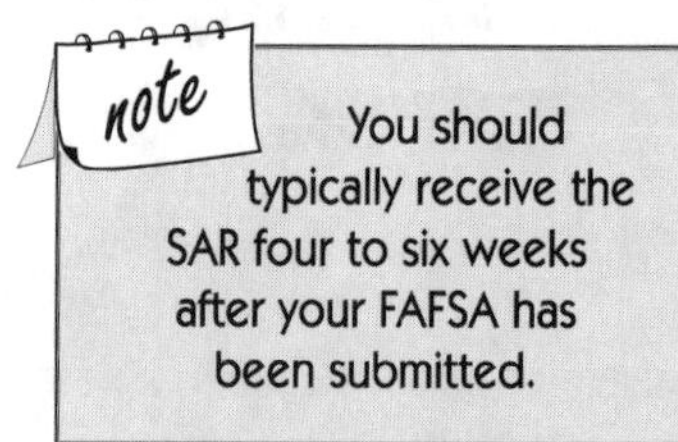

note
You should typically receive the SAR four to six weeks after your FAFSA has been submitted.

You should have a copy on file of the trial FAFSA that you ran in December. This copy will contain the figures you entered and the calculations that were made pertaining to your eligibility for financial aid. Compare the figures in your trial FAFSA to determine if the calculations by the government are what you anticipated. If there is a huge difference in the student and family's Expected Family Contribution you may wish to inquire as to why there is such a discrepancy by contacting the processing center.

Now is also the time to check the figures submitted with the original FAFSA and make sure they match the figures from the base year federal income tax returns of the student and the parents. Remember that estimates were acceptable in order to file your FAFSA on January 2nd; however, you must double-check to make sure the estimates were accurate. In the event your estimates were not completely correct, you will need to make the appropriate changes on the form provided with the SAR and return it promptly to the processing center. The address for the processing center is included in the SAR.

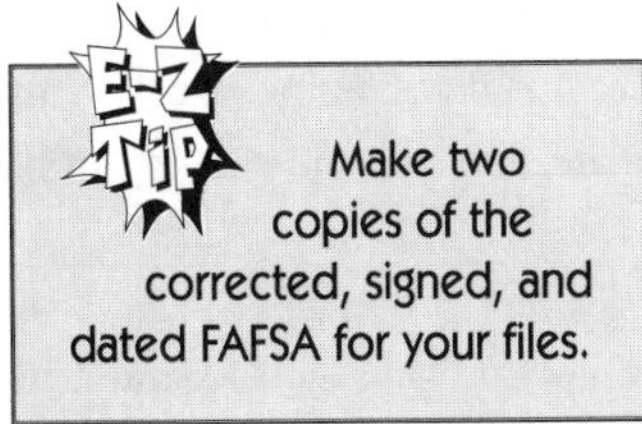

E-Z TIP
Make two copies of the corrected, signed, and dated FAFSA for your files.

Any significant changes in the student's or family's income and/or assets (loss of job, home, etc.) since the original filing of the FAFSA should also be noted on the corrections page of the Student Aid Report.

You will receive a corrected copy of the Student Aid Report back from the government in a few weeks. You should then mail a copy of the corrected SAR, along with a copy of the student's and family's federal tax returns and W-2 forms, to the financial aid office of each of your final six college selections. Send this SAR by regular mail and put it to the attention of the financial aid officer with whom you interviewed during your campus visit (if applicable). Although, the colleges will receive a copy of this information directly from the government, it is always best to be safe by also sending a copy yourself. This will ensure your aid package will not be adversely affected due to a misplaced or lost form.

If no corrections were necessary on your SAR, you may go ahead and send a copy, along with a copy of the student's and family's federal income tax returns and W-2 forms, to each of the financial aid officers at your selected colleges.

What to do if you are verified (audited)

The law obligates the federal government to verify financial aid eligibility for 30 percent of the students who receive some form of federal financial aid. In order to do this, the college will send you a verification form, requesting that you and your family provide documentation to substantiate your claims and figures you submitted for determining your eligibility for financial aid. These verification forms are standard and should not be cause for alarm.

The student and family should simply provide their federal income tax returns and W-2 forms for the base year of the financial aid application. These will often be all the documentation necessary to verify your eligibility for financial aid.

This verification process clearly shows how vital it is to make sure the data entered on the FAFSA is absolutely correct. It also shows the importance of keeping copies of all financial aid forms, tax forms, and correspondence when it comes to applying for college financial aid.

In addition to verification from the government, the college may choose to randomly verify your financial aid eligibility also. In fact, some colleges typically verify every student who is awarded financial aid. Again, there is no need to be alarmed; simply provide the college with the student's and family's federal income tax returns and W-2 forms for the base year of the financial aid application. This will typically serve as all the information necessary to verify your financial aid eligibility for the college.

Web-sites and phone numbers

In today's computer age there are countless web-sites available for the student and parents to reference information in regards to college selection and financial aid. Below are listed some of the most helpful web-sites and the general purpose of each:

www.ed.gov—the government's site with access to the FAFSA and answers to specific questions regarding different types of financial aid.

www.fafsa.ed.gov—direct access to the FAFSA.

www.finaid.org/calculators—financial aid calculator to estimate the student's eligibility for financial aid and determine an approximate Expected Family Contribution—EFC.

www.kaploan.com—further information regarding the calculation of the student's and family's Expected Family Contribution.

www.collegeboard.com—CSS/PROFILE application registration.

www.fastweb.com—free on-line scholarship search.

www.ecola.com/college—listing of over 2,500 colleges, with information and links to each.

In addition to the list of web-sites, please find below phone numbers and contact information for the FAFSA and CSS/PROFILE financial aid forms, as well as related information:

FAFSA—information center—(319) 337-5665

CSS/PROFILE—financial aid questions—(800) 778-6888

Federal Student Aid Information Center—(800) 433-3243

Student Aid Report—duplicate or lost—(319) 337-5665

Selective Service—(847) 688-6888

Social Security Administration—(800) 772-1213

College Answer Service—assorted student loan information—(800) 222-7182 or (800) 239-4211

FAFSA Express Questions—(800) 801-0576

Chapter 12

College campus visits

What you'll find in this chapter:

- Planning the college visit
- Meeting with the financial aid officer
- Parent's role in campus visits
- Exploring the campus
- Evaluating the campus

One of the most important things to remember while navigating the college preparation and funding maze is the fact that the entire process must be done in sequential order. The college campus visits are surely no exception to that rule. The campus visit is extremely important to the entire college preparation process because it lays the foundation for the relationship between the student and the college. In addition, it gives the student a chance to get a feel for the atmosphere of the college. Also, it allows the student to make that all-important "first impression" with both the college admissions officer and the college financial aid officer. During the campus visit, the college also gets its first chance to evaluate the student in person.

note

It would be nearly impossible for a student to make an attendance commitment to a college or university for four years without first getting an idea of the personality of the institution. The college campus visit gives the student an opportunity to visit with the students and faculty, and observe how the students live in the college environment. This observation and information will give the student an idea as to whether or not he/she would be able to achieve goals and academically prosper at that particular college.

Colleges across the country encourage students to visit their campuses. Colleges realize that a campus visit is by far the best way for the student to become familiar with the school. These campus visits give the college an opportunity to show their stuff to the students and at the same time gives the college a chance to further evaluate the student for possible enrollment.

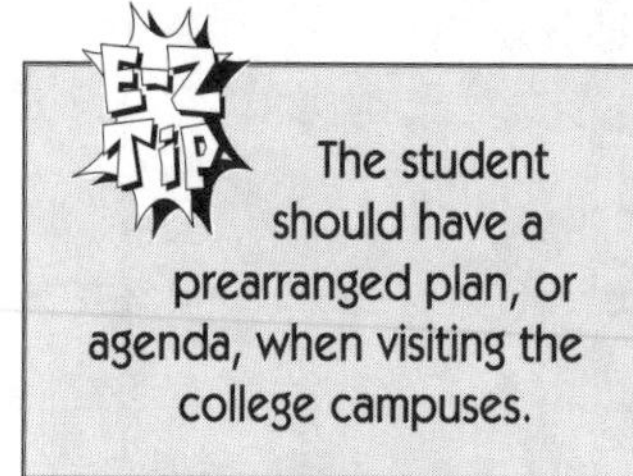

E-Z
TIP
The student should have a prearranged plan, or agenda, when visiting the college campuses.

Although colleges highly benefit from the student's visit, these visits should also be very beneficial to the students as well. There are certain things the student should observe; areas of the campus the student should plan on visiting; and people the student should make it a point to meet with. This chapter goes into great detail on the subject of who and what to see during the college campus visit. It also gives dozens of hints, tips, and suggestions regarding specific questions to ask and what to look for to make the campus visit as beneficial as possible.

After narrowing down your list of possible colleges to the six finalists (as outlined in Chapter 6), it is very important to visit as many of these top-choice colleges as possible. By completing the plans for these college campus visits early in the student's high school senior year, the process will be made much easier.

Originally, the student's list of possible colleges should contain 20 to 30 institutions. This list should then be narrowed to the student's six top-choice colleges, the ones the student will most likely apply to, and the ones the student feels they will excel at based on interests, wants, needs, goals, and accomplishments.

The college selection process is covered in much greater detail in Chapter 6, *College Search and Selection Process*.

E-Z TIP
The student should definitely visit these first six top-choices to get a clearer picture of what each school has to offer.

An important point to remember during the campus visits is the fact that college is definitely a buyer's market, and the student is definitely the buyer. Unless the institution is one of the few in the country that can literally pick and choose its students, the buyer (visiting student) should actually be in charge. However, it is extremely important the student only be aware of this information and then make sure to keep it to themselves. The student definitely doesn't want to visit the college campus with the attitude of "you need me worse than I need you." This type of attitude would not be beneficial for anyone, especially the student when it comes to the acceptance and financial aid process.

Although colleges know they need students, it is always best for the student to keep a professional and courteous attitude when visiting the college campuses.

When to begin the campus visits

Campus visits may actually be conducted starting during the student's high school junior year. However, the majority of students choose to visit the campuses during their senior year.

Using the first part of the student's senior year to make sure the campus visits are arranged and starting the visits in November is actually a very good practice. This will give the student time to carefully evaluate each and every one of his or her top six college choices. By planning the campus visits early, and arranging the visits effectively, a student should be able to visit all six top-choice colleges.

The planning and visiting of college campuses will take effort on the part of the student and the parents. However, it will more than pay off in the college final selection process—not to mention the financial aid package, and negotiation procedure, if applicable.

Best time of the week to conduct the campus visit

Although the student may have to miss a day or two of high school classes, visiting a college campus during the week is essential in order to get an accurate impression of the school. Classes will be in session, activities will be taking place, teams will be practicing, and students will be studying. These experiences will give the student the true feeling of the college.

As a general rule, visiting a campus on a weekend is usually a very poor practice. In fact, a weekend visit could hardly have any benefits at all. The admission staff and faculty will be gone for the weekend, and most of the students will be involved in other activities outside of day-to-day college life.

It is vital to visit the college campuses during the week. This is truly the only way to get an accurate impression of the school.

Staying overnight

The student should consider staying overnight at the college if at all possible. In fact, most colleges often encourage overnight stays. To arrange an overnight stay with a current student, you will need to contact the admissions office and make prior arrangements. It is good to stay with someone who has similar interests. For example: If you will be playing football, ask the admissions office if it would be possible for you to stay overnight with a football player. An overnight stay will certainly give the student a much better feel for the entire college atmosphere.

An effective campus visit

Making good use of your time during the campus visit is essential. There are actually three ways to explore the college campus. Effective campus visits should contain all three methods, which are:

1) Planned appointments arranged with the admissions officer and the financial aid officer.

2) Guided tours, usually conducted by a volunteer or work-study student.

3) Personal observations through a self-guided tour.

Planned appointments with admissions and financial aid officers

First of all, the most important part of the campus visit is to meet with the admissions officer and the financial aid officer. These pre-scheduled meetings will set the foundation for the college's evaluation and acceptance of the student, as well as start the student's financial aid file. Beginning a conversation with these officers during the campus visit is vital.

> **HOT spot** Remember the student is making a first impression, an impression that may weigh heavily during the admission and financial aid process.

The student should call and/or write ahead to arrange a meeting with both the admissions and financial aid officer. The call, and/or letter, should be courteous and contain the expected dates for the student's visit. The student should inform the officers of the visit and ask for a brief meeting to introduce himself/herself.

Meeting with the financial aid officer

During the campus visit, and subsequent meetings, the student should be prepared to briefly discuss the following information with the financial aid officer:

- the family's financial condition
- the family's ballpark net worth
- the parent's general income range
- any money that has been saved for college expenses

This discussion with the financial aid officer will allow him or her to at least give the student an idea of the possible financial aid package that will be offered by the college, and to become familiar with your particular situation, and make notes to your file. This will be very beneficial down the road in the financial aid process, and the appeals process, if necessary.

The meeting with the financial aid officer should be short and to the point. The main purpose of this meeting is to personally introduce yourself, and to make a favorable first impression.

Remember when it comes to your financial aid package, the financial aid officer will have the final say. He or she will be dealing with thousands of students he/she knows by only a name and number. For the officer to be able to put a face with the name, and hopefully have a favorable impression of you, could make a world of difference when it comes to awarding financial aid.

Meeting with the admissions officer

During the meeting with the admissions officer you basically have two goals:

1) to tell the college about yourself

2) to find out all you can about the college

In meeting with the admissions officer, the student should familiarize him or her with the student's goals, aspirations, and achievements. Keep in mind that the admissions officer is usually very busy, and the purpose of this meeting is to make that good first impression, briefly discuss a few of the student's achievements, and find out all you can about the college.

The interview with the admissions officer is a chance for both of you to ask and answer questions. You are asking questions that will give you a feel for what the college has to offer, and the admissions officer is trying to convince you that his institution is the right one for you to attend.

It is important that there be an equal balance between you asking questions about the college, and giving the college information about yourself.

The interview with the admissions officer could have a far greater effect on your acceptance to that particular institution than a 20-point difference in your SAT score. The interview with the admissions officer is a very important part of the college campus visit process, and should be treated as such.

Important things to know about the interview:

- Don't ask unnecessary questions—in other words, questions you should already know the answers to.

- Show self-confidence when talking about yourself and your achievements.
- Be polite and courteous, never pushy or overbearing.
- Try to relax.

What you should bring with you to the interview:

- A list of the questions you wish to ask, including:
    - ✧ Can I receive college credit for advanced placement courses I take while still in high school?
    - ✧ How many freshman courses do graduate students teach?
    - ✧ What is the typical class size?
    - ✧ Will I be able to earn my degree in four years?
    - ✧ How secure are the dorms?
    - ✧ What are the most important factors the admissions officer takes into consideration in determining a student's application?
    - ✧ Do I get advice from professors on which courses I should take?
    - ✧ Do fraternities and/or sororities play a big part in campus life?
    - ✧ What different sources of financial aid may be available?
    - ✧ What are the possibilities of my being accepted?

- a copy of your high school transcript
- a pen and paper for taking notes
- a friendly, outgoing personality

It is important to dress casually during your interview. There is no need for a suit and tie; however, short pants would not be appropriate. Dress neatly, clean cut, and portray a positive self-image.

Items about yourself that you should review with the admissions officer during your interview:

- high school courses you have taken
- any activities you participated in during high school
- positions you have held in high school
- outside jobs you have had
- particular areas that interest you and could possibly become your college major

In addition, you may wish to briefly mention some of the other colleges and/or universities that you have visited.

Probably the most important part of the interview itself is honesty. In fact, if the admissions officer suspects you are not being truthful in any way, you essentially have no real chance of being accepted.

E-Z TIP: Being honest with the admissions officer about who you are and what you have achieved will certainly go a long way towards your acceptance.

Parent's role in the campus visits and interviews

Parents should accompany the student on all campus visits and during the all-important interviews, if at all possible. Although it will ultimately be the student's decision, the parents should be there to offer support, opinions, and possibly catch a few things the student may overlook. The parents are often able to give another perspective.

HINT

Although parents are in attendance, the student and parents should always remember one thing—this is the student's interview—not the parent's. It is true that three pairs of ears can surely hear more than one; however, the interview should be between the admissions and financial aid officers and the student. The parent's main purpose is to give the student support, and listen to the discussions closely for later comparison with the student's notes.

Be sure to pick up all necessary applications and forms before leaving the admissions and financial aid offices.

After the interviews

The notes the admissions and financial aid officers take during the interviews will be placed in your file, a file that was created when you originally requested information from the college. This file will also contain your application for admission, which is covered in Chapter 7. The officers will refer to your file when it is time to make the all-important admission and financial aid package decision. Their decision for your admission, and eventual financial aid package, will be based primarily on your application,

> **HOT spot** It is extremely important that both the financial aid officer and the admissions officer remember you as someone who would benefit their institution.

your situation, your goals, your achievements, and your personality. The first impression you make during your interviews will go a long way towards the determination of your acceptance and ultimately, your financial aid package.

Guided tours of the campus

Most generally a volunteer or a work-study student will conduct a guided tour, a general tour around campus. Common stops along the way include:

- the library
- the cafeteria
- the dorm, or similar housing
- the student center

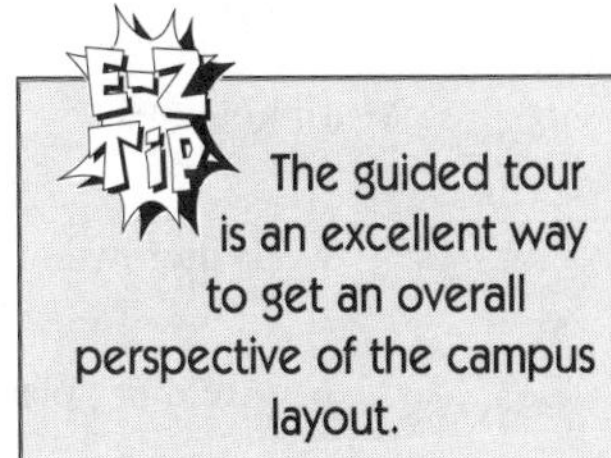

The guided tour is an excellent way to get an overall perspective of the campus layout.

If there are particular parts of the campus that are not included in the tour, you may simply ask the guide for directions and they will usually help you locate it. This type of campus tour usually lasts around an hour. Feel free to ask the tour guide questions, either during the tour or after the tour is over.

The guided campus tour is strictly for your benefit. Always feel free to ask any questions that you may have.

Your self-guided campus tour

Even though the guided tour may give you an overall impression of the campus, you will still need to further investigate aspects of the college on your own. Again, you should remember to spend your time wisely when exploring the following areas of the campus:

- Classroom—you may either pick a class from a schedule obtained through the admissions office, or you may pick a class at random that interests you.
    - How big is the class?
    - Are the students enthused about the subject/lesson?
    - Read over the class syllabus, if available.
    - Can you picture yourself as a part of this class?
- Visit the library
    - Is it crowded, comfortable?
    - Are quiet places available for study?
    - Can you picture yourself there for four years?
- Visit a particular department that interests you and talk with a student in that major and/or a professor in the department.
- Make a visit to the athletic facilities.
    - Are they crowded?
    - Are trainers available for you?
    - Is all of the equipment relatively new?
- If you will be involved in sports, go to a practice or game. Talk to the coach and/or players if possible. Does the team seem like one that you would like to be a part of?
- Visit the freshman dorms.

    - ✧ How big are the rooms?
    - ✧ Are they comfortable?
    - ✧ Are the bathrooms adequate, clean?
    - ✧ Where are the laundry facilities located?

- Eat a meal in the cafeteria.
    - ✧ Is the food good; is there a wide variety?
    - ✧ Is it crowded?
    - ✧ Are the people/students friendly?
- Check to see if there are receptive people in the student services and writing centers to help you.
- Visit the student center and talk with several different students to gain their opinion of the facility.
- Take a short trip off campus and see what the surrounding area is like. Check to see if there is adequate shopping and suitable restaurants nearby.

In addition to visiting the above listed locations, and talking with the people to get a genuine feel of the college's atmosphere, here are a few things you may do to give you a further indication of the type of college life at each particular institution:

- Read the school newspaper and discover the hot campus topics and the general concerns of the student body.
- Review the bulletin boards to see what type of events and organizations are advertised.

- Investigate what the weather is like, and if it is a climate that is appealing to you.

- Feel free to take pictures of the campus and write down any impressions you may have for future reference.

All of this information may be very helpful when it comes to making your final college selection.

It is vital to send a thank you note to everyone you talked with during each particular campus visit. You should take the time to write a short note or letter thanking them for their time and the pleasure of meeting with them, and allowing you to discuss your possible future at their particular institution.

Your evaluation of each individual college campus

Your findings during the college campus visits will not be as useful if you are unable to clearly document your findings for future reference and comparison. In fact, notes from your campus visits will prove very valuable when it comes time to make your final college choice.

Directly after the campus visit is the time to score each college based on your findings. You should create a file for all of the campuses that you visited, complete with the following information and ratings (where applicable) for each:

- college size and location

- time and date of your visit and the weather conditions

- annual college cost including tuition, fees, and room & board

- the type of institution: public, private, religious, 4-year, college, university, etc.
- student body general profile: friendly, smart, dressy, casual, diverse, spirited, etc.
- social life: student initiated, college sponsored, clubs, sports oriented, etc.
- housing: dorms, apartments, fraternity, sorority, etc.
- recreation and activities: team sports, intramural, gym facilities, music, drama, etc.
- services: health, career, employment, etc.
- library: good, adequate, fair, poor, etc.
- outside community: easy access, city, town, rural, etc.
- academics: relaxed, modern, small classes, large classes, etc.
- faculty: full time, part time, Ph.D's, etc.

You may assign a rating, or grade, for each of the above listed topics, and then an overall rating (superior, good, adequate, or disappointing) to the institution. You should also make notes as to what you liked most about the college and what you disliked.

All of this information should then be placed into your file which has been created for each college. This information file will be used during final college choice decision time to help aid you in making your final selection.

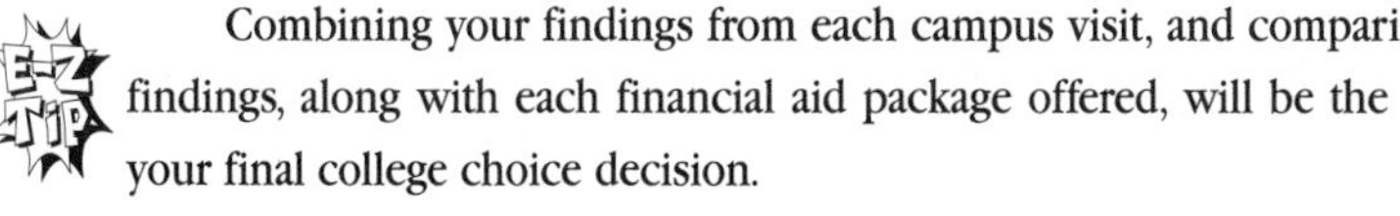

Combining your findings from each campus visit, and comparing those findings, along with each financial aid package offered, will be the basis for your final college choice decision.

Although campus visits are time-consuming and take careful preparation and planning, they will prove very valuable farther down the line. Remember that the college preparation and funding procedure is a highly sequential process. Thorough campus visits are a vital and necessary part of this sequential procedure. Be sure to make the most out of your college campus visits; the effort will surely pay great dividends.

Chapter 13

What to do before making your final choice

What you'll find in this chapter:

- On-campus housing deposits
- College admissions offers
- Financial aid award offers
- Private scholarship notification

There are several items that now must be done prior to the selection of your final college choice. You should familiarize yourself with all of these tasks. They will take place during March, April, and May of your high school senior year, and are extremely important details that must be taken care of in order to navigate the college preparation and funding maze effectively.

You have spent hours and hours researching, making notes, applying, studying, reviewing, and now is the time all of that hard work will begin to pay off.

During the spring of your high school senior year you will receive the results of all your hard work in the form of college admission acceptance letters, financial aid award letters, and (hopefully) private scholarship award letters.

On-campus housing deposits

The first thing you should do, usually in March, is make sure that you pay all necessary on-campus housing deposits at your six finalists colleges or at least, request an extension until after you have made your final college choice selection. Most institutions will grant you an extension, but you must make sure you contact each individual college or university and request the extension first. It is vital that you have housing reserved if you choose that particular institution as your final selection.

You should write the admissions office of each institution to request your housing deposit extension. Be courteous and professional in your request and you should have no problem in obtaining an extension. Following up your letter with a phone call for prompter attention is usually a good policy.

If the institution will not grant an extension (some schools' policies will not allow them to) you should make sure you pay the necessary deposit(s) prior to the due date to ensure you will have housing. It is also important to check to see if the housing deposit is refundable, and what steps are necessary to obtain the refund. Colleges know that high school students are now in their final college selection process, and the institutions usually have provisions for the cancellation and refunds of on-campus housing deposits.

College admissions offers

Sometime in late March or early April, you will begin receiving the letters of acceptance from each college to which you applied. (Hopefully you will be accepted by all six of your finalist colleges; if not, there is no need to be overly concerned.) This has been a long wait; remember that you submitted your original admissions applications back in October. However, your patience has finally paid off.

All your hard work, the advanced placement classes, the activities which you actively participated in, the narrowing of your possible colleges and the research involved with that, your submitting an effective admission application—now begin to pay dividends.

Typically, if a student applies to six colleges, he/she will usually be accepted at four or five of them, depending on each one's enrollment criteria, the student's achievements, and the way those achievements are portrayed to the colleges on the admission application. If you are not accepted at all six of your finalist colleges, do not be alarmed, it is very common. Remember that is why you applied to your four top picks (in order), a long shot, and a safety valve, as outlined in Chapter 6, *College Search and Selection Process*, and Chapter 7, *College Admissions Applications*. The more colleges that offer you acceptance, obviously the more options you will have in making your final college choice, which is outlined in Chapter 16.

The acceptance letters will come directly from the college's admissions office. In addition, you will also need to know another very vital piece of information before you will be able to make your final college choice selection—the financial aid package. There are several different methods used by colleges to notify you of your financial aid award package. A few institutions will include the information with your admissions acceptance letter, while most schools will send you a separate "award letter," usually within one to four weeks after mailing your admissions acceptance letter.

Before you can even begin to make your final college choice selection you must first receive each college's financial aid award package. Even if you know that one of your possibilities is at a state university where you will be able to pay for your education without much financial aid, and you have been accepted by that university, you should wait before making your final decision. Remember that you have spent years preparing yourself for college, and literally weeks making the appropriate applications to your final

> **HOT spot** It is vital to first see what each school offers you prior to making your final college choice.

six college choices. Now wait to see how all your hard work will pay off in the college's eye by evaluating each financial aid award offer prior to making your final selection.

Most all of the college's admissions acceptance letters you receive require that you acknowledge and accept the offer by signing and returning the letter, or a copy, or another similar form. You should sign and return the necessary paperwork to the college's admissions office as soon as possible. You should also make sure that by signing you will not be obligated to attend, and that you may relinquish your spot on their campus if that institution is not your final college choice.

We realize that no institution will force you to attend, but we are more concerned with any deposits that may not be refundable, etc. It is best to have the cancellation and refund policies known upfront to be on the safe side. Relinquishing your offered admittance is usually not a problem at most colleges—they realize that you still may be in the decision-making process, and have provisions for students who change their minds.

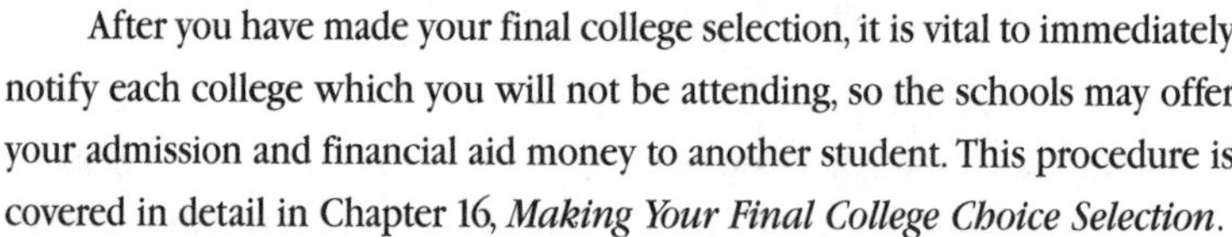

After you have made your final college selection, it is vital to immediately notify each college which you will not be attending, so the schools may offer your admission and financial aid money to another student. This procedure is covered in detail in Chapter 16, *Making Your Final College Choice Selection*.

Financial aid award offers

In addition to receiving an acceptance letter from each college, you will also receive an "award letter," usually under a separate cover, approximately one to four weeks after receiving your acceptance letter. The reason the award letter often comes separately from the acceptance notification letter and takes a few weeks to receive is because the college's admissions office must notify the financial aid office of your acceptance. The financial aid office must then put together your financial aid award package. This is where all the hard work you have done to this point really begins to pay off. The financial aid office and officer you visited during your college campus visit will now pull your file and determine the amount of financial aid the institution will offer you. It is important to remember that the college must first distribute the government's money (grants, work-study, and loans) as instructed; however, the institution then has the option of making you a financial aid award offer for any or all of the remaining financial need which you may have. Your work and dedication in high school, along with your campus visit and interview with the financial aid officer, and the effective admission application you put together will now have a direct effect on how much financial aid you are offered.

> **HOT spot** Remember, many colleges (especially private institutions) have the ability to offer as much financial aid as the student needs.

The award letter you receive from each college will contain the amount of financial aid you are being offered if you choose to attend that particular college or university. Your award letter will contain all the financial aid that is offered by both the federal government and the institution itself. (Any financial aid you may receive in the form of private scholarship money is usually not included in your award letter from the college. This type of financial aid, and the acceptance and placement of it, is covered later in this chapter, as well as in Chapter 9, *Scholarship Application Process*.) Your award letter will include all types of financial aid: federal grants, federal work-study, institutional grants and scholarships, and possibly some loans.

Evaluating and negotiating (if applicable) of each award letter is covered in detail in Chapters 14, 15, and 16 and will be a vital part of your final college selection decision.

It is vital that you immediately sign and return all award letters that you receive from the colleges, acknowledging acceptance of the awarded financial aid. The financial aid you are offered by the college and the government is not valid until the college's financial aid office receives your signed acceptance. Sign the award letter, keep a copy for your records (and later comparisons), and return the original to the college's financial aid officer immediately.

The student should immediately sign and return all college award letters (which outline their financial aid award offer) to the college's financial aid officer to validate their award.

After you have determined your final college choice you will be able to notify each school that you will not be attending and relinquish your financial aid award. The institution will then be able to offer your financial aid to another student. It is vital, however, to first accept each and every award you receive and then later turn down the offers from the schools that you will not attend.

Private scholarship notification

In addition to receiving financial aid from the federal government and the colleges themselves, you may also receive aid in the form of scholarship money from private scholarship sponsors to which you have applied. (Scholarship sources and the scholarship application process are covered in Chapters 8 and 9.) In the event you do receive a private scholarship, you will receive an award letter stating the amount of the award, the terms and conditions of the award, and instructions on what you must do to obtain the awarded money.

The student should immediately send a letter of acceptance to the scholarship sponsor, addressing it personally to the person whose name appears on the award notification letter. In addition, the student should also follow up the acceptance letter with a phone call (three or four days after mailing the acceptance letter) directly to the scholarship sponsor's office and personally thank the sponsor for the award. During the acceptance and thank you call, the student may also wish to inquire as to when the awarded funds will be distributed and if there are any other details that must be completed before the funds may be received.

A personal thank you and acceptance letter, along with a follow-up phone call, will not only ensure that the student has accepted the award, it will also lay the foundation for future awards from that particular scholarship sponsor. Remember that financial aid is awarded annually and must be re-applied for each and every year. Although past recipients sometimes have priority when it comes to future awards, it never hurts to keep your foot in the door for any scholarship funds that may be available further into your college career.

HOT spot It is vital to have your scholarship money replace funds you would otherwise have to borrow or work for.

When you receive a scholarship, it is important to make sure the amount of the award is deducted from the self-help aid (work-study and loans) portion of your financial aid package. Some institutions will attempt to take your scholarship money off your gift aid (grants and other discounts) instead of deducting it from your awarded self-help aid.

If the college or university is not willing to deduct your private scholarship funds directly from your self-help aid, at least make sure both your self-help aid and gift aid are reduced equally by your scholarship. Please refer to Chapters 10 and 11 regarding more detailed information on the positioning of the financial aid package awarded funds.

Conclusion

HINT

By paying attention to the details outlined in this chapter and taking care of all the odds and ends, you will then be able to move on to the next step of the college preparation and funding maze. Next, you will begin evaluating the college's award letters, negotiating those award letters (if applicable), and ultimately making your college final selection determination. Remember, you worked hard and spent years to get to this point; it is vital to now pay close attention to all details in order to take full advantage of your accomplishments and hard work.

Chapter 14

Evaluating college award letters

What you'll find in this chapter:

- Institutional Student Information Report (ISIR)
- Creating your award letter
- Effectively comparing award letters
- Types of financial aid
- How to organize award letter data

The colleges you listed on your Free Application for Federal Student Aid, or FAFSA, will automatically receive a report from the government. This report, which is called the *Institutional Student Information Report*, or ISIR, details your eligibility for federal aid. The information contained in this report is basically the same information that is included in the Student Aid Report, or SAR, that you receive directly from the government after filing your FAFSA.

Institutional Student Information Report

The ISIR will include any aid that you are eligible for from the federal government. The government determines your eligibility through its calculations of the data that you provided in your FAFSA. Common types of financial aid awards that are included in the ISIR are as follows:

- Federal PELL Grant
- Federal SEOG Grant
- Federal Stafford Loan
- Federal Perkins Loan
- Federal Work-Study Program

Creating your award letter

The colleges then take the information they receive from the government and create their financial aid offer to you. This offer is commonly known as the *package*, and comes in the form of an *award letter*. The award letter not only contains the federal financial aid you are eligible for, but it will also include the financial aid the college is offering you. The colleges are mandated to distribute the government's financial aid as instructed; however, they are free to distribute their own financial aid as they see fit. This allows the colleges to attract the students they want, in order to build the college community they desire.

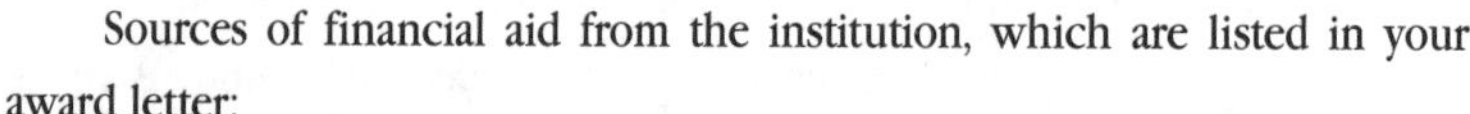

Sources of financial aid from the institution, which are listed in your award letter:

- Institutional Grants, or Tuition Discounts
- College's Private Scholarships

In addition, the college's award letter will also list the following annual estimated expenses:

- Tuition/Fees
- Room/Board

- Books/Supplies
- Personal
- Transportation
- Medical

By totaling these expenses, the student and the parents will have an estimate of the total cost of attendance for that particular college or university for one year. By then deducting the Expected Family Contribution from the total cost of attendance, the student and parents will determine the student's *demonstrated need.*

DEFINITION

The student and parents may then add up all the financial aid awards offered and hopefully this amount will be equal to the student's demonstrated need. If the amount of the financial aid offered is less than the demonstrated need, this balance must also be paid (in addition to the Expected Family Contribution) by the student and parents in order for the student to attend that particular institution.

note

Be sure to check the EFC figure on your award letter as compared to the EFC figure that was included in the Student Aid Report you received from the government. The EFC is located in the upper right hand corner of the SAR and should match closely with the figure contained in the award letter. If there is a significant difference, the financial aid office should be contacted immediately.

Preferential packaging and gapping

There are two very important terms that you should be familiar with when it comes to college award letters. They are *preferential packaging* and *gapping.*

First, *preferential packaging* simply means that the most attractive students receive the most attractive financial aid offers. This clearly shows the importance of making sure the college is completely aware of all the student's high school achievements. The student's financial aid awards will be directly affected by how attractive they are to the colleges and universities. Details on how to make your high school accomplishments "shine" are covered in Chapter 4, *Preparing Your High School Transcript*, Chapter 7, *Application to Colleges*, and Chapter 12, *College Campus Visits*.

The second term is *gapping*, which means the aid package offered you by the college does not meet your full need. For example: If your financial need is $10,000 and your award letter from the college only contains an offer of $8,000 in financial aid, then you know that you have been gapped. Gapping is an immediate signal that the college is not concerned whether the student chooses to enroll with them or not. Gapping may also be the basis for the student's appeal for additional financial aid. The appeal and negotiation process is covered in Chapter 15. Obviously, a financial aid award letter that contains no gap proves to be far more attractive.

Double-check all figures and totals on the award letters

It is important for the student and family to double-check all figures and totals on the college award letter. An error could have occurred when the government forwarded the financial aid eligibility information to the colleges, or when the college produced the award letter. It is extremely important to catch an error of this nature as soon as possible, and begin steps necessary to correct any such mistake by immediately contacting the college's financial aid office.

Compare the Student Aid Report figures with the amounts listed on the award letter and make sure the two match.

Accepting all financial aid offers

It is very important to immediately accept all financial aid offered in your award letter. You may do this by signing and returning the award letter to the college's financial aid office.

Always be sure to keep a copy of all correspondences with the college.

You have the option of accepting only certain parts of the award letter; however, that is not advisable because you may always pick and choose your final award at a later date. For example: If you decide you need more time to study and cannot work as much as required by the federal work-study portion of your award, you may wish to decline the work-study program. It is very important that you wait and make that determination later. At first, it is vital that you accept all forms of financial aid. This will reserve the aid in your name and keep the colleges from offering your awarded financial aid to someone else.

Always accept all financial aid offers immediately by signing and returning the college's award letter to their financial aid office as soon as possible.

Effective comparison of award letters

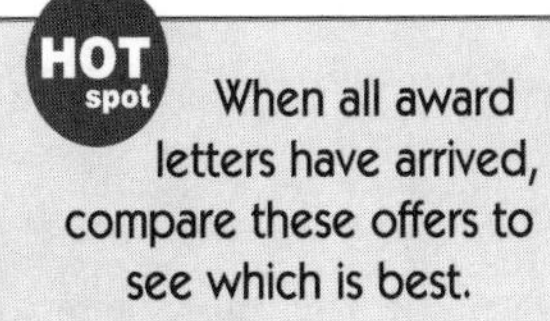

HOT
spot
When all award letters have arrived, compare these offers to see which is best.

It may take a few weeks for all the student's award letters to arrive. Remember the student should have listed six colleges on the FAFSA, and each of those colleges will make the student a financial aid offer in the form of an award letter.

When evaluating six different colleges' award letters, it is common for the top two or three to be very similar and very competitive with each other. Sometimes it is hard to pick a clear favorite or winner. Each has distinct advantages. Remember that this is not the only aspect of the final college selection process. It is only a portion of it. Evaluate the financial aid award letters fairly and thoroughly and enter that information into each college's file. There are several other factors to be taken into consideration when making your final college choice and these award letter evaluations will be included in those findings. The other items to be considered are covered in detail in Chapter 16, *Final College Choice*.

HINT

There are several items that must be taken into consideration when it comes to comparing college award letters. Those items will be covered in detail in this chapter and are as follows:

- Amount of gift aid offered and the percentage of gift aid in comparison to the total financial aid package.
- Amount of self-help aid offered and the percentage of self-help aid compared to the total financial aid package.
- Has the college offered an institutional grant/tuition discount?
- Comparison as to the percentage of gift aid and self-help aid offered.
- Has the college or university met your full financial need? Has gapping occurred?
- Is the college's appeal policy listed on the award letter, and, if so, what is it?

This award letter comparison process is simply the evaluation of each individual financial aid offer and a determination as to which college is offering the best award package. This is not the student's final college selection. The student should evaluate this award letter information and create a file for each college, just like he or she did with their findings during the college campus visits, covered in Chapter 12. The student will later need to determine the final college choice, and the award letter evaluation information will be included in that decision, along with the campus visit evaluations, and each individual school's reputation, as well as the student's personal preferences and notes.

The evaluation and comparison of the award letters is another step along the way in achieving the student's goal of the highest quality of education at the most affordable price.

Gift aid

Gift aid is defined as any financial aid that the student does not have to work for or pay back. It is simply a gift, and includes the following:

- Grants—which may come from the government or the college.

- Scholarships—which come from the colleges.

These scholarships are college awards and not outside scholarships from a separate organization. Those outside scholarship awards are most generally not included in the student's award letter, and will be deducted from the expected family contribution, or the gap in the financial aid package, if applicable.

- Fellowships—awarded by the colleges.

Obviously, the more gift aid offered by the college, the better. The student should determine what percentage of the total financial aid package is gift aid. He or she may do this by dividing the total gift money offered by the total financial aid that is awarded. This percentage will be very important in determining the desirability of the college's financial aid offer.

The next section in this chapter will help the student determine the percentage of self-help (loans and work-study) aid offered. The student will then be guided in drawing a comparison between the amount of gift aid and self-help aid.

Self-help aid

Self-help financial aid is money that is either worked for or borrowed. Self-help aid includes:

- work-study jobs
- loans

The more self-help aid offered in the financial aid package, the less attractive the package becomes. The student will either be obligated to work while in school, or pay back the loans, usually after graduation. The more gift, or free, money that can be obtained to start with, the less the student will have to repay.

Most students are either involved in the federal work-study program while attending college and/or borrow money to attend. In fact, 60% of college students borrow some amount of money to attend school. In 1997 the average borrower owed $17,000 upon completion of four years of college.

Although it is true that the student may need to work while in school, or borrow money to attend, the amount of this type of financial aid should be kept to a minimum whenever possible. This factor makes it very beneficial to accurately assess the college award offers and determine which will be the overall best scenario for the student.

The student should now total the amounts of self-help aid offered and determine what percentage of the total financial aid package is loans and work-study. He or she may do this by dividing the total amount of self-help aid by the total aid offered.

Has an institutional grant been offered?

An *institutional grant* is another form of financial aid. Although this type of grant is relatively new in the financial aid market, it is becoming more and more common.

In some cases the college will include as a part of the financial aid package an institutional grant, often called a tuition discount. This type of award is just exactly that, a discount off the college's published price of education.

Private colleges and universities with a larger endowment fund are typically the ones that offer an institutional grant. Public schools and state universities commonly do not have the funds necessary to make these type of lucrative financial aid offers.

Institutional grants are usually given to the students that the college is determined to enroll. They are actually used as an incentive for these students. Remember that all colleges want good students, and they are more than happy to enroll the top students by offering them a discount off the advertised cost of attendance. This again shows the importance of making sure that the student's achievements are accurately portrayed to the colleges. Chapters 7, *Application to Colleges*, and Chapter 12, *College Campus Visits*, give detailed outlines on how to make the student's credentials shine for the colleges.

Comparison of gift aid versus self-help aid

Typically, a well-balanced financial aid award letter will have an equal percentage of gift aid and self-help aid. Remember that the more gift aid, the better.

In comparing college financial aid award letters, the ratio between gift aid and self-help aid is valuable information. The higher the ratio of gift to self-help aid usually indicates the anxiousness of the college to enroll the student. Remember that colleges generally must distribute the government's money as instructed and then use their own resources to build the college community they want. If the government offers a small amount of financial aid in the form of gift money, or grants, the college still has the option of offering its own funds in the form of an institutional grant, or tuition discount.

Remember, only certain colleges and universities have adequate funds to offer students discounts in the form of institutional grants. You must first determine if the institution is able to offer a grant. Your findings should be included in your evaluation of the school. Commonly, private colleges and universities offer these types of discounts, and state and public institutions are unable to make these types of offers because of their limited funds. If the college has a high percentage of students who are receiving financial aid and if the gift-aid ratio is high compared to the self-help aid, and also the cost of attendance, it is most likely the college is able to negotiate.

Government grants are usually need based and if the student and family's assets prevent the student from having a huge need, the grants will often be minimal.

Has gapping occurred?

Determining what percentage of the student's full financial need has been met by the college is vital. To do this, simply compare the total cost of education for one year (minus the EFC) with the amount of financial aid offered. If there is a remainder for the student and/or family to pay, then gapping has occurred.

Always remember that award letters are often computer generated and a financial aid officer of the college will not see the majority of the award letters prior to their delivery. The government's computers have determined your aid eligibility and then, in most cases, the college's computers have interpreted and passed that information on to you in the form of an award letter. To date, there has still been no personal involvement in the determining of your financial aid package.

It is vital that the student includes the financial aid officer in the award process. The college campus visit, discussed in Chapter 12, outlined how to properly interview with the school's financial aid officer. You may now use the opportunity to cultivate what you have planted. Involving the financial aid officer could make thousands of dollars worth of difference in the amount of financial aid you receive. This follow-up and possible negotiation with the financial aid officer falls under the *Negotiation of the College Award Letter*, which is covered in detail in the next chapter, Chapter 15.

Remember, if there has been a significant gap discovered in your award letter, negotiation may be an option; follow the steps outlined in Chapter 15 to successfully navigate this portion of the financial aid maze.

The appeal policy

Most college award letters will contain the college's appeal policy. This is valuable information in the event that an appeal is pursued. In the event an appeal is necessary, a great deal of time and effort will be saved if the appropriate appeal procedure is followed.

HOT spot The student should review the appeal policy to become familiar with its terms and procedures.

Details on negotiation and the appeals process is covered in the next chapter.

Gathering and organizing award letter data

In order to effectively compare each award letter and find the overall best financial aid package, the information must be organized into a useable format. The information should be arranged side by side, where it is easily compared. All information and figures included in the award letter should be listed on the comparison sheet.

Remember that comparing "apples to apples" is very important. In other words, make sure your comparison sheet is uniform—this will ensure a fair evaluation of each individual offer.

The following data should be included in your award letter comparison sheet:

- Total costs of college for one year—including tuition, room, board, fees, books, supplies, transportation, medical, and miscellaneous expenses.
- Expected Family Contribution—EFC—listed on the award letter and should be double-checked against the Student Aid Report amount, which is received from the government.
- Student's Financial Need—this may be determined by subtracting item 2 from item 1, above.
- Gift Aid (Free Money)—total the amount of gift aid from all of the following sources: Scholarships, Federal PELL Grant, Federal SEOG Grant, State Grant, Merit Grant, Need Grant.

- Self Help Aid—total the amount of self-help aid from all of the following sources: Federal Perkins Student Loan, Federal Stafford Student Loan, other student loan, campus job/federal work-study, miscellaneous.

- Determine the total amount of financial aid awarded by adding the total of item 4 and item 5, above.

- Include the ratio from gift-aid to self-help aid.

- Determine the gap, or unmet need, between the awards and the student's demonstrated need by subtracting the total financial aid package, 6 above, from the total financial need, 3 above. (The total financial need is the amount arrived at after the family's EFC is deducted from the total cost of college.) For example: If the total cost of school for one year is $25,000 and the family's EFC is $2,000; then the financial need is $23,000. If the total financial aid award is $20,000; then the total gap, or unmet need, is $3,000.

By arranging all of the above information into a chart that allows for side by side comparison you will be able to clearly determine which financial aid offer is the best.

You may now plug the data for items 1 through 8, from the previous pages, into our example of an effective college award letter comparison chart as follows:

	College A	College B	etc.
1) Total Cost of College			
2) Expected Family Contribution			
3) Student's Financial Need (subtract 2 from 1)			
4) Total Gift Aid			
5) Total Self-help Aid			
6) Total Financial Aid (add 4 and 5)			
7) Ratio between Gift and Self-help Aid			
8) Gap between Total Financial Aid and Demonstrated Need (subtract 6 from 3)			
9) Total Money Needed (add 2 and 8)			

The top two or three colleges' financial aid award offers may be very similar and very competitive, with each having its own particular strengths.

Determination of best financial aid award package

There are two main factors to consider in evaluating the college award letter:

1) The ratio of gift-aid to self-help aid.

2) The gap between the total awarded financial aid and the student's demonstrated need.

Students must also take into consideration the amount of time each college's work-study (if applicable) job offer requires each week. A college freshman may well need additional time for studies and getting familiar with the everyday workings of the college environment. Any extra time that may be needed for a work-study job may be somewhat harmful in the long run. Usually a work-study job that requires less than 15 or 20 hours a week is acceptable for a college freshman.

HOT spot Securing a work-study job in your selected field of study could prove very beneficial after graduation.

Employers like to hire employees (graduates) who have experience in the field.

note

Remember, any money that is offered in the form of grants is not only free money, it is also money that will probably be in the form of loans at another institution. For example: Let us say a student receives a $5,000 grant and a $5,000 loan from college A, and a $7,000 grant and a $3,000 loan from college B. College B's offer is far better due to the fact that the student not only gets more free money from college B to start with, he or she also has $2,000 (plus interest) less to pay back after graduation. It is a double bonus. The student benefits both at the time of enrollment into college and again upon graduation, and probably for many more years to come.

After the award letter information is organized and compared, the student and family must determine which offer is best. The following questions should be taken into consideration when evaluating the college's financial aid award letters:

1) How much gift aid is offered by each institution?

2) Is a tuition discount offered, and if so, is it adequate compared to the history of the college's financial aid offers?

It may be beneficial to first negotiate for additional gift aid (if applicable) in the form of a tuition discount before the final determination is made regarding the best financial aid package.

3) How much self-help aid is offered by each institution?

4) How much do the student and/or family want, or can afford, to borrow for a college education?

5) How much does the student want to work while attending college?

By comparing the information contained in the award letters in a manner outlined in this chapter, and considering the five previously listed questions, the student and family should be able to make a final determination as to the best financial aid award package.

This determination is not the student's final college choice selection. There are many other factors that must be considered before that decision can be made. The information covered in this chapter simply allows the student to have additional information in the file that will prove very beneficial when it comes time to make the final college choice decision. Determining the final college choice is covered in Chapter 16.

How funds are distributed

After the student signs and returns the award letter to the college (keep a copy and return all award letters promptly—you will be able to later decline the colleges that you will not attend), the award letter will be valid.

It is vital to immediately accept all awards offered by the colleges. In order to do this the award letter must be signed and returned as soon as possible.

E-Z TIP
Negotiating for additional financial aid (if applicable) may be done after the award letter has been returned and validated by the college.

The college's financial aid office will then notify the business office of your awarded funds. All funds (except for the work funds, which have not yet been earned) will be credited to your account, which is often referred to as the student bill. You will later receive your student bill for all of your college expenses and the financial aid awards will show up as a credit on the bill. You will be responsible for any balance after the financial aid awards have been credited.

Chapter 15

Negotiating college award letters

What you'll find in this chapter:

- Circumstances that warrant an appeal
- When and how to negotiate
- How to write appeal letters
- Negotiating for additional financial aid

> **note** Negotiating a college award letter is a relatively new method for obtaining additional financial aid.

Even though colleges are becoming more consumer-oriented, and most colleges are now aware of the fact that negotiating is becoming more and more popular, negotiating still must be done very professionally and very tactfully. Having the attitude that the college owes the student more money and will automatically be forced to negotiate is not beneficial for anyone, especially the student and the family. Any negotiating tactic that may be used to obtain a more attractive financial aid package should always be handled very delicately.

The student and family should have a specific strategy for negotiation. This makes the negotiation process much more effective. There are commonly two circumstances that may serve as a foundation for a financial aid package negotiation.

One of these circumstances is if something changes in the lives of the student and/or the parents after the FAFSA has been submitted. In the event the student or family incurs an illness, divorce, loss of job, damage to their home, or any similar instance, this may surely be a cause for the amending of the original financial aid offer.

The second time the student and family may negotiate for a better financial aid package is when the college makes the student an offer in the form of an award letter, and the student and parents do not totally agree with the amount of financial aid that has been proposed.

E-Z TIP

Probably the most important factor involved in this type of negotiation strategy is to determine if the college is able to negotiate in the first place. Most colleges will usually state their appeal and negotiation policy in the student's award letter. As a rule, private institutions are generally the ones that do negotiate. They have a much greater endowment fund and have access to more surplus capital, which may be used for financial aid. Public universities and colleges are generally not able to negotiate (however, some will) because of their limited funds and restrictions placed on them by the government.

A financial aid officer at a public college would need to waive the government's rules in order to negotiate the financial aid package. This does happen sometimes, but is not generally a common occurrence. On the other hand, a financial aid officer at a private college or university is able to be much more liberal with financial aid due to the fact that it is actually the institution's own money.

Circumstance 1: A major change in the life of the student and/or the family

If something in the student's life changes it may be cause for the financial aid package to change also. After filing for financial aid, if the student and/or family incur an illness, divorce, loss of job, damage to their home, or any similar instance, this may surely be a cause for the amending of the original financial aid offer from the college.

It is, however, the sole responsibility of the student and the parents to provide this information to the college's financial aid officer in a timely, professional, and convincing manner. The information must be explained in specific terms. The financial aid officer must be aware of the entire situation and convinced that the situation warrants a change in the financial aid package.

The student and parents should review the following information. Any of the items listed below may provide grounds for which an appeal for more financial aid would be appropriate. For example:

- Does a brother or sister of the student attend a private school for any type of learning disability? If so, the financial aid officer should be notified because this type of information is not included on the FAFSA or CSS/PROFILE financial aid application.

- Are the family's budgeted expenses much higher than normal for such items as diet, health, transportation, or disability?

- Does the student receive Social Security benefits? If so, these usually will be cut on the student's 18th birthday and should be brought to the attention of the financial aid officer.

- Does the student's family provide, or pay for, nursing care for an elder member of the student's family? This information should be also reported, as it is not listed on the FAFSA or CSS/PROFILE application.

- Has a divorce or separation occurred after the original financial aid forms were filed?

- Has a death occurred in the family since the original financial aid forms were filed?

- Has a parent lost his or her job since the filing of the original financial aid forms?

- Does the family experience a bad credit history, and are they limited to the amount they may borrow for college? If so, notify the financial aid officer of this information.

- Does a parent plan to retire during the student's college school year?

- Do the parents plan to have another child while the student is in college?

- Has there been damage from fire, or flood, or any similar occurrence to the family's home that will require money to repair?

E-Z TIP

If any of the previous scenarios apply, it is very important to notify the financial aid officer of the college immediately. These items are usually not listed on any financial aid application forms, and if the information is not passed on to the college's financial aid officer, he or she has no way of knowing the circumstances faced by the student and the family. The financial aid officer may offer the student more financial aid; however, they must first know the reason why it is necessary.

The student may wish to call the financial aid officer with this new information. The student should also follow up the phone call with an appeal letter. (Examples of appeal letters are located towards the end of this chapter.)

If the college or university is near the student's home, or it is convenient for the student and parents to visit the school, the appeal information would be much better conveyed in person. A trip to visit the college's financial aid officer with this new information could literally make thousands of dollars worth of difference in the student's financial aid package.

If the appeal for more financial aid is made in person, it is a good practice to also provide the financial aid officer with a letter of appeal that may be placed in the student's file.

This also further shows the importance of spending time during the college campus visits to talk with and make that all-important good first impression with the financial aid officer of the college. This good first impression will always prove very valuable down the line, especially in the event that negotiation for a better financial aid package is pursued. Visiting with the financial aid officer and what to do during the college campus visit is covered in detail in Chapter 12.

The financial aid officer will make the determination of whether or not to amend the original financial aid offer. "Professional judgement" is the common term used to describe the financial aid officer's decision. If he or she feels that the situation warrants a change, by awarding more financial aid, they have complete power to make that change.

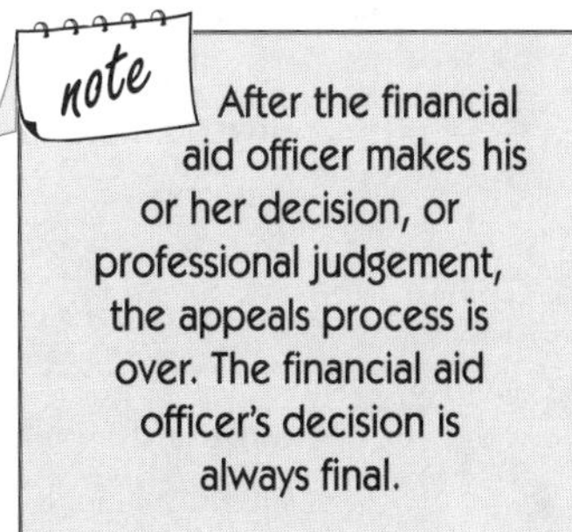

note
After the financial aid officer makes his or her decision, or professional judgement, the appeals process is over. The financial aid officer's decision is always final.

Circumstance 2: Negotiating for a tuition discount

The second instance where negotiation for additional financial aid would be appropriate is much different than the first. The student and family may negotiate for more financial aid if they think the college is simply charging the student too much for attendance. To determine this, research into the financial aid history of the college and the college's typical financial aid package must be done. This may be accomplished by reviewing the college's financial aid information located in a college directory or at the College Board's web-site, which is located at *www.collegeboard.org*.

If the college has a high percentage of students who are receiving financial aid and if the gift-aid ratio is high compared to the self-help aid, and also to the cost of attendance, it is most likely the college is able to negotiate.

As a general rule, most private colleges and universities are able to negotiate, and most public institutions are not. However, it is best to investigate each college or university separately to determine their negotiating ability.

In addition to this research, there are several other factors that may be taken into consideration by the student and family to determine the ability of the college to negotiate. The following are questions the student and parents should ask themselves, not the college. For example:

- ✧ How do the college's costs compare with similar colleges around the country?
- ✧ Is the college's enrollment down? Do they need students?
- ✧ What is the college's history in their mix of financial aid between self-help aid and gift aid?
- ✧ Is the college in need of minority enrollment? If so, and you are a minority, you may take advantage of this situation.
- ✧ Does the college seek the enrollment of National Merit finalists? If so, and the student is a National Merit finalist, he or she may take advantage of this situation.

✧ What percentage of the total enrollment receives financial aid?

✧ What particular special talent is the college currently seeking?

When to negotiate

DEFINITION

If any of this research shows the college will typically negotiate, or the college is in the need of the student's particular qualifications, the student and parents may then ask for more financial aid, effectively a reduction in the college's published cost of education. This reduction is typically called a *tuition discount*.

Financial aid comes in many different forms. The student and parent must be able and prepared to take advantage of all types of financial aid that is available. Whether it is a tuition discount or a scholarship from an outside source, it is still considered financial aid. No matter where this financial aid comes from, any money that is contained in the student's financial aid package is money the student and family will not have to pay towards the cost of the student's education.

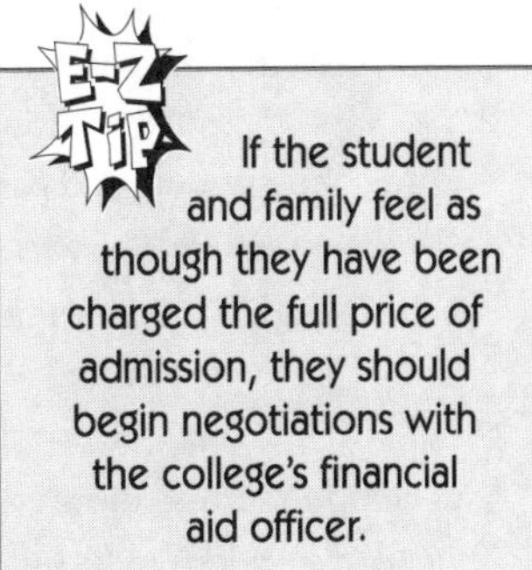

E-Z TIP
If the student and family feel as though they have been charged the full price of admission, they should begin negotiations with the college's financial aid officer.

Keep in mind only about 35 percent of first-year students are actually paying the college's full sticker price which is listed in most college directories.

How to negotiate

Although being charged the full price for the cost of admission is surely a reason for negotiation, this type of negotiation must be handled very differently than if they are negotiating because of a sudden change of circumstances. Even though the colleges are very aware of the negotiation of financial aid, it is still a very touchy subject. This type of negotiating can be delicate. However, it could literally make thousands of dollars worth of difference over the course of an entire college education.

In this second type of negotiation the student and family are, essentially, asking for additional financial aid only because they want it. In the first scenario, they were asking for more financial aid because there had been a drastic change in their situation and they needed more financial aid to make up for their misfortune.

This second type of appeal may also be handled with a phone call directly to the financial aid officer, and then followed up by an appeal letter. (Sample appeal letters are found towards the end of this chapter.) However, an appeal for more financial aid is often better received by the financial aid officer in person. A trip to the college and a personal, scheduled meeting with the financial aid officer could well be worth the time.

It is always best to draft a letter of appeal and deliver it to the financial aid officer personally during your scheduled meeting. Please ask that the letter be placed in the student's file.

The student and parents must approach the financial aid officer with the proper attitude. The "can you help us out" approach will always work far better than "we got a better offer somewhere else, can you beat it?"

One very effective method of approach is by asking for suggestions or help in meeting the student's financial aid obligations. This will often lead to a conversation, and a much more receptive financial aid officer. If the student and parents are able to convey the fact that all of their financial aid possibilities have been exhausted and the student may be forced to study at a less expensive college they will have a much greater chance of receiving additional financial aid.

> note
> Most financial aid officers are willing to help a sincere student who is genuinely concerned with his/her financial aid package and the quality of education.

During the appeal for additional financial aid the student and parents may also wish to review the student's high-school achievements with the college's financial aid officer. This must also be done professionally and tactfully. The student and parents do not want to overwhelm the financial aid officer with the student's accomplishments. Instead, they want to simply reiterate the student's individual qualities, and show the financial aid officer how the college would benefit from having the student on his or her campus.

E-Z TIP

Actually holding back one of the student's specific achievements, and using it during the negotiation stage may be very beneficial. Purposefully omitting a minor achievement by the student and then later bringing it to the attention of the financial aid officer may persuade him or her to offer more financial aid.

The college's financial aid officer always has the final say in determining the student's financial aid package. He or she may use their own discretion when it comes to awarding financial aid based on how the college feels about the student, and how much they would like the student to attend.

The financial aid officer can always work for you; make sure you keep him/her on your side. It is always best to make an appeal for more financial aid in person. However, if that is not always possible, a phone call directly to the financial aid officer, along with a follow up appeal letter would be the next best thing.

Even if a personal meeting with the financial aid officer is scheduled, it would be good to also bring your appeal letter to the meeting with you.

The most effective appeal letters are generally written by the parents and should contain the following information:

- ✧ student's name, phone number, and social security number
- ✧ purpose of the letter
- ✧ reason for the appeal (reduction of income, etc.)
- ✧ a tactful comparison of a different college's financial aid offers (if applicable)

The following two financial aid appeal letters show how to construct an effective appeal and/or negotiation strategy:

Appeal letter 1 – Change in student and/or family financial condition since the original application for financial aid was filed

January 1, 2000

Mr. Financial Aid Officer
ABC University
123 Forth Street
Atlanta, USA 12345

Subject: Letter of Appeal, Loss of Family Home
Re: John E. Student, SSN 123-45-6789
Phone: (123) 456-7890

Dear Mr. Financial Aid Officer:

I write to inform you of our family's tragic loss. Last week our home caught fire and completely burned to the ground. We were all very fortunate;

none of our family members were hurt in the fire. However, all of our belongings and valued family possessions were completely destroyed.

After checking with our insurance company, we discovered that there were many items not covered by our homeowner's policy. It is going to be very costly to find a new home, and replace the valuable items our family lost.

I sincerely hope you will be able to take this new disheartening information into consideration and reevaluate my son's financial aid need. Both John and I would greatly appreciate it.

Thank you for your time and what you have already done for John, and our family. If you should have any questions, please feel free to contact us. We look forward to hearing from you concerning this matter.

Sincerely yours,

John, Sr.
Father

This appeal letter is direct and to the point—it certainly gets the message across. Again, the financial aid officer can do nothing to change the aid package unless he or she is aware of the new circumstances in the student and family's life.

It is always the sole responsibility of the student and parents to make sure the financial aid officer has a complete knowledge of the family's financial situation, or any change in it.

Appeal letter 2 – Appeal for additional financial aid based on a lack of sufficient income

January 1, 2000

Mr. Financial Aid Officer
ABC University
123 Forth Street
Atlanta, USA 12345

Subject: Financial Aid Appeal Letter
Re: John E. Student, SSN 123-45-6789
Phone: (123)456-7890

Dear Mr. Financial Aid Officer:

Please find enclosed my signed award notification from your institution. I have some questions and concerns, and I am writing for your guidance.

I have a younger brother and a younger sister who will also be attending college during the next six years. My parents and I have reviewed our family budget and my parents are concerned they will not be able to support me during my college days at ABC University. Our budget is almost $5,000 per year short. Might you possibly assist my family and I in identifying other sources of financial aid that we may have missed? Any ideas or help that you may offer would be greatly appreciated.

Thank you for your time and what you have already done for me. If you should have any questions, please feel free to contact us. We look forward to hearing from you concerning this matter.

Sincerely,

John E. Student

This financial aid appeal letter is asking for help. Remember to always work with the financial aid officer, not against him/her. He/she will surely make an effort to help the situation, given the fact the appeal letter is structured professionally and worded tastefully.

Never try to bully the financial aid officer or force him/her into negotiations. This tactic simply will not work, and will make for hard feelings between the student, the parents, and the college's financial aid officer.

Additional financial aid award information

Should the student receive an outside scholarship or similar award, it is important to know how the college or university will position that financial aid in the student's financial aid package. Most colleges and universities will attempt to immediately deduct this awarded amount from the gift-aid offered by the institution. It is vital that the student and family make sure the student's award is reduced equally with respect to the work study and/or loans and the tuition discount in the event the student receives an outside scholarship.

Summary

Although negotiating with the colleges and universities is a relatively new method of achieving a more lucrative financial aid package, it can be very effective. The key point to remember is to be tactful and professional in your appeal and do not simply assume the college is forced to negotiate with you.

It is true that a college financial aid officer works for the college. However, they are also concerned with seeing students get their all-important college degree. Practically every financial aid officer is willing to work with the student and the family to ensure the student receives the highest quality of education.

Remember, having the college financial aid officer on your side is the key. Without that, negotiating for additional financial aid will be painstaking, to say the least.

Chapter 16

Your final college selection

What you'll find in this chapter:

- How to arrange research and aid award offers
- Rank and compare your six finalists
- Your final college choice selection
- Important post-decision items

Decision time has now arrived. You have spent hours researching possible colleges. You and your family have attended college fairs, and made campus visits to each of your finalist institutions. You have taken notes, created files, arranged information, and now it is time to review your findings. You have narrowed your list from hundreds of original possibilities down to six finalists and now you must pick the one college that is best for you from that list of six finalist institutions.

The student should welcome the advice and input from parents, friends, his or her high school counselor, and anyone else who figures into the scenario. However, it is important that the final decision ultimately be that of the student's.

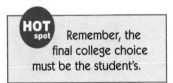

> **HOT spot** Remember, the final college choice must be the student's.

To allow you to make your final college choice selection as effectively as possible, you will need to arrange all of the information you have gathered to date and compare these findings side-by-side. This will allow the student to determine which college is best for him/her. By arranging the information into a side-by-side format and taking all things into consideration the student will be able to make a well informed decision.

This final college choice decision will obviously be the foundation for the student's college education and degree and will also have a great determination on the student's career and ultimately the student's future. The decision of selecting the final college choice is probably one of the biggest of the student's life and should be given careful consideration and adequate time.

The final college selection decision process should actually begin in April of the student's senior year of high school.

Before preparing the notes and paperwork necessary to make the final college choice decision, the student must first wait to receive all letters of acceptance from the colleges and also the financial aid award letters from each individual institution that is offering the student admittance. This procedure is covered in Chapter 13.

note

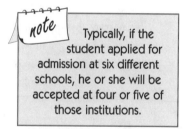

Typically, if the student applied for admission at six different schools, he or she will be accepted at four or five of those institutions.

The student's acceptance for enrollment depends largely on the college's enrollment eligibility requirements, the student's high school achievements, and how those achievements were portrayed to the institutions. It is important to apply to six different colleges, as outlined in Chapter 7, in order to give the student several different options.

For the student to apply to only one or two colleges and then be denied admission at those institutions would be disastrous.

After the student receives the letters of acceptance (or unfortunately denial in some cases) from the colleges, along with the college's financial aid award letters from the institutions offering admission, is the time to begin the comparison of the colleges. The colleges will most likely make their decisions sometime in April regarding the student's admission and the information (acceptance letters and award letters) from the institutions will be mailed shortly thereafter to the student.

Gathering information necessary to make the final decision

In order to make the most informed decision, the student should begin by gathering and arranging all the information that has been collected to date regarding the six finalist colleges:

- All campus visits information, including personal notes and any scores assigned to each individual campus.
- All financial aid packages that will be outlined in the "award letters" that are received from the finalist colleges offering the student admission.
- Notes on the college's location, enrollment size and overall appeal.

Arranging college campus visit information

In Chapter 12, *College Campus Visits*, you were given an outline of effectively evaluating each of the individual college campuses you visited. This information was then to be placed in a file for future reference. You should now compare your ratings from each campus visit, and created file, in order to arrange your colleges in order of preference. The highest rating, the college that had the most overall appeal to you, should be ranked first, with the second favorite being ranked next, and so on. After the schools have been arranged in order, based on your campus visits, it is time to now incorporate your financial aid offers from each institution into the final college choice scenario.

Arranging the financial aid package award offers

Each of the colleges or universities that offered you admission will send you an award letter that outlines your financial aid package at that particular institution. This award letter will contain all financial aid you have been awarded by the federal government as well as the financial aid offered by the institution itself.

Any financial aid that you have been awarded by a private source, such as a private scholarship, is generally not included in your award letter from the college. You will generally be notified of these awards directly from the scholarship sponsor and it is the student's responsibility to make sure the award(s) are acknowledged and accepted, as well as making sure the funds are received.

You should now arrange your financial aid award letters in a similar manner to which you arranged the information gathered from the campus tours. You should determine which financial aid award package is best for the student and rank it as the number one offer, determine which is second, and so on. The amount of total financial aid versus the amount of the student's "need," along with the amount of gift-aid (grants or commonly called "free-money") versus the amount of self-help aid (work-study and loans) will help you determine which financial aid package is the best.

College location, enrollment size, and overall appeal

Finally the student should arrange any notes he or she may have concerning the six finalist colleges. These notes and/or information should include the location of the college, the enrollment size, and the student's overall impression of the institution.

Ranking your final college selection

Now that you have arranged all of your information regarding your finalist colleges and assigned a ranking for each specific topic, it is time to do a side-by-side overall comparison to find your final college choice.

The ideas and procedures outlined in this chapter, along with the entire guidebook, are not intended to influence your decisions while selecting a college in any way, shape, or form. We are simply outlining procedures (based on proven methods and results) which you may follow, that may help you by saving you time and money. We realize that the college preparation and funding process is confusing, and by putting our strategies and step-by-step procedures to use, hopefully any indecision you may have will be eliminated. In addition, we hope the information you gather from this guidebook will assist you in making the most informed decisions possible. We trust that the strategies and ideas outlined in this chapter, and this guidebook, will help you a great deal; however, remember that the final college selection decision will ultimately be yours.

The determining of your final college choice will, and should, take some time. There are many variables to consider and as is often the case the top two or three colleges are very close when it comes to determining your final selection. In fact, one college may be better in a certain area than the next school, but the second school may offer something else that is a little more attractive than the first.

In order to evaluate which institution is best, the student must first determine what is important to him or her. The student may do this by listing in order what qualities, and characteristics he/she is looking for in a college. Undoubtedly, the amount of financial aid awarded is going to be at the top of the list. Besides the financial aid package, we have listed below several other items that the student may take into consideration when determining what is most important to him or her in looking for the best college. The student should write down these items, in order from most important to least, by using his/her own notes and ideas along with some of the suggestions we have listed below:

- The institution's enrollment size and location.
- If the student moves away from home, how often does he/she want to be able to visit?
- Is on-campus housing important or does the student wish to live off campus?
- Is the campus safe?
- Can the student receive a degree in four years from this particular institution?
- How large or small are the classes?
- Will the student's Advanced Placement courses be applied towards college credit at this particular institution?
- Are the faculty members friendly?
- Are most of the classes taught by professors?

- Are the advisors receptive and eager to help?
- Are the students people he/she would feel comfortable with?
- Is the institution one where he/she could excel and prosper?

By arranging a list of the items that are most important to you, you will then be able to effectively evaluate each college in your finalist list and make the determination of your final college choice.

Now plug in your findings and notes from each individual college with the list of what is most important to you and you will be able to see which institution is best suited for your future educational needs.

College comparisons

For example, let's say the top three items you are looking for in a college are:

- financial aid package
- enrollment size
- being within 300 miles of home in order to visit your family three or four times a year

You plug each college's information into these particular criteria and determine which one is best suited to accommodate your needs. If the top two or three choices are still very close after considering this information, you essentially have two other options which may help you make your final decision:

1) You may either want to go down to your next two or three important criteria and compare the institutions further.

2) You may wish to take into consideration your overall feelings and impression of each institution and make your final choice from that information.

Either way of further evaluating these colleges is effective and is a matter of preference for the student.

In the process of choosing your final college choice, it is vital to keep your options open and gather and arrange as much information possible in order to make the best possible selection. Remember that this selection will have a direct bearing on the student's future and should be made with great care and commitment.

After the final choice

The final college choice decision has been made and it is now time to move on with other important items which must be completed in order to ensure the student will be ready to begin classes in the fall at the college or university he or she has selected. We have listed these items (in order) for you:

1) Financial Aid Offers. The student and parents should make sure that the financial aid offers are accepted and submitted to the final college choice. You may do this by double-checking to see that the college's award letter has been signed and returned to the institution. When the school receives the signed award letter from the student, the financial aid package is valid.

2) Submit a copy of the Student Aid Report (SAR), along with a copy of the student's and parent's federal tax returns and W-2 forms. The student and parents should forward this information, via certified mail, to the financial aid office of the college. You may wish to address your information to the attention of the financial aid officer that you interviewed with during your campus visit. The college's financial aid office may already have some, or all, of this information,

but it is always better to be safe than sorry by making sure the institution has all the necessary paperwork in order to admit the student.

3) On-campus housing paperwork and deposits. The student should request any paperwork necessary for on-campus housing (if applicable) from the college's financial aid office and/or admissions office. The student should immediately fill out this paperwork upon receipt from the college and submit, along with any required deposits, the forms by certified mail.

4) Paperwork for student loans (if applicable). The student and family should obtain from the college's financial aid office forms that may be necessary for any applicable student loans. These may include the Federal Stafford Loan, the Federal Perkins Loan, and the FPLUS parents loan. The student and parents should then complete their sections of the loan application(s) and return them by certified mail to the address provided with the application(s).

5) Notify the non-selected colleges. The student should notify all of the colleges which were not selected and inform them of the fact that the student has chosen not to attend and is relinquishing their earlier financial aid acceptance. (This is very important because the financial aid that you are turning down will then be offered to another student.) The student should write a letter to each of the college's financial aid offices and keep a copy of the letters for his/her records.

6) Final high school grade transcript. The student should obtain and forward a copy of the final high school grade transcript to the admissions office of the college. (The college may already have received this information directly from your high school; however, again, it is better to be safe than sorry.)

In addition to the above listed items, if the student is awarded a private scholarship, he or she must make sure the awarded funds are received and credited properly towards their college cost of attendance.

After all of the listed steps have been completed, the student should now be ready to begin college in the fall. The student was able to find the best college to meet his or her educational needs, and a college where the student can prosper and receive the highest quality of education available.

Chapter 17

Beginning your college freshman year

What you'll find in this chapter:

- Meeting with the financial aid officer
- Scholarship search for sophomore aid
- Renewing FAFSA and CSS/PROFILE
- Reviewing & processing the SAR
- College's award letter for sophomore year

As the student begins freshman year there will be several things to do. Most of these details are involved with settling into college, getting comfortable with new surroundings, and beginning work on the college degree. In addition to the day-to-day activities of the college freshman, and all of the new responsibilities to now face, the student also has a few details that must be covered in the college preparation and funding maze. If the student takes care of these details, it will make the entire transition from home life to college life a little easier.

This chapter serves as a checklist and reminder of the items that the student must do during freshman year. These items are not that involved, and there are actually only a few of them.

You can relax in knowing that the majority of the work is now over. What you went through during your high school years in preparing for and selecting a college, along with the applications for financial aid and admission, were far more complicated and time-consuming than what you now face as a college freshman. The foundation has all been set; you are now in college. The majority of your time should be spent in adjusting to your new environment and concentrating on making the most out of the educational opportunity that you have created for yourself.

This chapter covers a few basic items that you should make note of and be sure to follow-up on; they are basically renewal forms, along with a couple of odds and ends.

Remember that financial aid is an annual event and must be applied for as such; however, the renewal application(s) are usually much easier and far less time consuming than the originals.

Meet with financial aid officer

August – First of school year

At the beginning of your freshman year of college, hopefully during the first day or two you spend on the campus, you will be able to meet with the college's financial aid officer. You should have met him or her during your college campus visit, and perhaps have written or spoken to him or her since that time in regards to your financial aid package.

During your meeting with the college's financial aid officer you should reintroduce yourself and make sure to mention the fact that you are still searching for any future financial aid awards such as scholarships or fellowships that may be offered by the institution. It always pays to stay in touch with the financial aid officer and remember that he/she can, and will, work for you. Keeping them on your side is vital.

A good working relationship with the college's financial aid officer is always valuable to have. It will usually pay dividends in the long run.

Remember that you are going to be at this institution at least four years and you want to make the financial aid part of your stay as convenient as possible.

In your meeting with the financial aid officer, you should also discuss the details of your work-study job (if applicable), which is part of your financial aid package. You will want to get the specifics on your job, the total hours you will be working each week, and any other questions which you may have concerning your work-study program.

Taking the time to meet with the financial aid officer will be time well spent. Stop by his or her office and make an appointment for a brief meeting. The financial aid officer is very busy, especially at the start of the new school year. Keep your meeting direct and to the point. Thank him or her for their continued help and be courteous and professional during your meeting. You will be glad you took a few minutes out of your schedule to make a brief visit to the financial aid office.

Scholarship search

October - December

We have mentioned several times in this guidebook that the government's and the institution's financial aid packages must be re-applied for each year. Financial aid from private sources through scholarships is no exception to this rule. They are also an annual event.

There is one big difference in private source scholarships and the government's and college's financial aid funds: the private source scholarships vary (there are hundreds of new scholarships available each year) and the governments and colleges pretty much stay the same. This means that you have already done the necessary footwork to locate the sources of aid from the government, and obviously the college itself; however, you should continue to search for new scholarships for which you may qualify during your freshman year of college. In fact, to continue to keep your scholarship file open and continue searching for new and additional sources throughout your entire college career is a very good idea.

Be sure to keep a list of any scholarships which you may have already received. You will probably need to reapply for the award next year, or at least show the sponsor proof that you are still attending college so that you may receive the financial aid scholarship amount the following year.

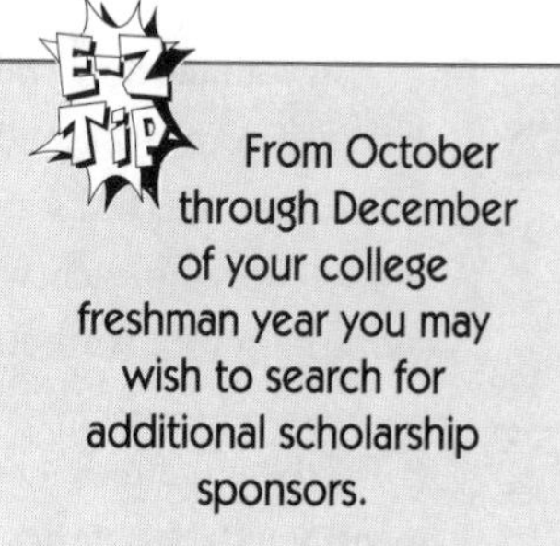

E-Z TIP
From October through December of your college freshman year you may wish to search for additional scholarship sponsors.

In your search for additional scholarship sponsors you may wish to refer to Chapter 8, Scholarship Sources and Availability, as well as Chapter 9, Scholarship Application Process. You may want to run an on-line "free" scholarship search from some of the sources listed in Chapter 8, and also conduct a local search for additional scholarship sponsors. It is also a good idea to mention to your college's financial aid officer that you are in the market for any new available scholarships. Tell him/her to keep you informed of any new scholarship opportunities that become available. This again shows the importance of staying in touch with the college's financial aid officer.

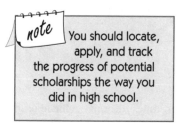

> *note* You should locate, apply, and track the progress of potential scholarships the way you did in high school.

Once you have compiled your new list of possible scholarship sponsors, you should follow the steps outlined in Chapter 9, Scholarship Application Process, in order to apply effectively for those new scholarships which may be available for the next school year (your college sophomore year).

Renewal FAFSA & PROFILE (If applicable)

December - January

During December of the student's college freshman year both the student and the parents should gather, arrange, and prepare the necessary information to file the renewal FAFSA (Free Application for Federal Student Aid) and, if necessary, the CSS/PROFILE financial aid application.

It is true that renewal applications for financial aid do have priority over new applications; however, it is still vital to file your financial aid applications as soon as possible after January 1st. In this guidebook you learned, and should always remember, that the single most important factor in the financial aid application process is that aid is always on a first come, first served basis. Renewal financial aid is no different. You must remember that there is a limited amount of financial aid available each year; the financial aid "pot" does run out. It is vital to always be at the front of the financial aid line. This will ensure that you receive your fair share of the available funds, and you will not be shorted because you failed to file your application on time.

The renewal FAFSA will be much the same as the one you filed last year unless there have been drastic changes in the student's and/or the parent's lives. (For example: divorce, death, loss of job, loss of family home, etc.) In general, if everything remains relatively the same in the student's life, his or her renewal application for financial aid (FAFSA & CSS/PROFILE) will be much the same as the previous years.

Please refer to Chapter 10, Financial Aid Sources, and/or Chapter 11, FAFSA and CSS/PROFILE Applications for any questions you have in regards to filing your renewal application(s) for financial aid.

Remember to file your renewal FAFSA on January 2nd. This will ensure that you are first in line for financial aid, and you will not miss out on this available aid because you failed to file promptly.

Student aid report - SAR

February - March

In February or March of your college freshman year you will receive the results of your FAFSA (Free Application for Federal Student Aid) which you filed on January 2nd.

This will come in the form of a Student Aid Report, or SAR. The student and family should take the time necessary to review the Student Aid Report and make sure all the figures are correct and coincide with the amounts that were on the FAFSA application. If there are any mistakes or items that need to be corrected, because of a change in the student's, and/or parent's life since the filing of the FAFSA, they should be made immediately. The student should then return the corrected Student Aid Report to the central processing center. The address of the processing center should be listed on the SAR.

The student should wait for the corrected copy of the SAR to come back from the government and then forward, via certified mail, a copy to the college's financial aid office. If the original Student Aid Report was correct, and there was no need to make any changes or corrections, the student should then forward a copy of the original SAR to the college's financial aid office. Again, it is always best to send the SAR via certified mail.

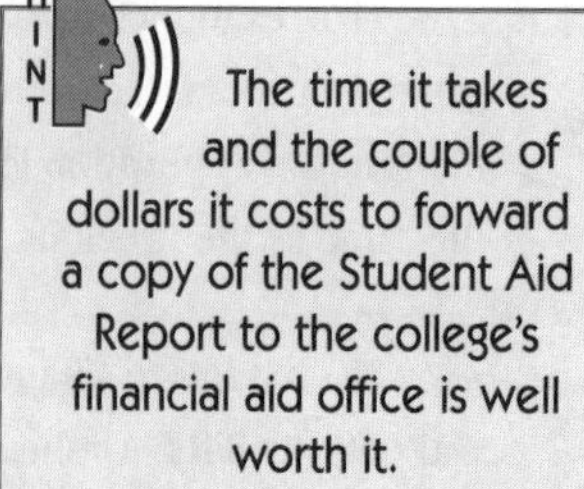

HINT
The time it takes and the couple of dollars it costs to forward a copy of the Student Aid Report to the college's financial aid office is well worth it.

We realize that the government will send a copy of the SAR, which is called the Institutional Student Information Report (ISIR) directly to the college; however, remember that it is always better to be safe than sorry.

You may refer to Chapter 10, Financial Aid Sources, or Chapter 11, FAFSA and CSS/PROFILE Applications, for any further questions you may have regarding the filing of your financial aid renewal applications.

During February and March the student should also continue to track the progress of his/her scholarship searches. You may wish to run another on-line "free" scholarship search, and/or perhaps a local scholarship search, to look for new sponsors who may be able to provide additional financial aid for your next school year.

Award letter for college sophomore year

April - May

After the college's financial aid office receives the copy of the Student Aid Report from you and/or the Institutional Student Information Report from the government, it will begin arranging your financial aid package for your college sophomore year. This package will include financial aid from the federal government, as well as aid from the college itself.

The college will then forward its financial aid offer to you in the form of an "award letter." You should take the time to review and compare the awarded financial aid with last year's amount, making sure that you receive all financial aid that you are eligible for, and/or have received in the past.

After you have reviewed your financial aid award letter, if everything is correct, you should then accept it by signing and returning it to the financial aid office. You may also write a separate acceptance letter (if necessary), enclose a copy of the award letter, and then return them both to the college's financial aid office. Again, it is important to mail these via certified mail to ensure that the financial aid office receives them and you have a copy of the delivery.

As with all important correspondences with the college, be sure to keep a copy of the documents for your records.

If you should have any further questions regarding the evaluation and/or acceptance of your college award letter, you may refer to Chapter 14, Evaluating the College's Award Letter.

In addition to the Award Letter, the student should also forward to the college's financial aid office, via certified mail, a copy of both the student's and the family's federal income tax returns from the previous year, along with the applicable W-2s.

In April the student should also now spend some time to arrange his or her final list of possible scholarships and begin making applications to each of those sources. You should also track the progress of each scholarship application over the next few months. You may refer to Chapter 9, *Scholarship Application Process,* for further details.

Conclusion

This chapter served as a checklist regarding the items that the student must do during his or her college freshman year to receive the maximum amount of financial aid available for the following school year.

As you can see, this list is relatively short compared to the list that was covered during high school. Again, the foundation for your financial aid package was set during your high school years; all you need to do now is reapply in a timely manner, and closely monitor the progress of your renewal financial aid each year.

Chapter 18

How to receive maximum financial aid

What you'll find in this chapter:

- Understanding "gapping"
- Negotiating you financial aid package
- Changes in your financial picture
- Reducing the cost of a college education
- Checking out "discounts"

Up to this point in the guidebook we have given you step-by-step procedures to help you successfully navigate the college preparation and funding maze. Hopefully you now have a much better idea of what you are facing when it comes to preparing and applying for college, as well as obtaining financial aid to help pay for your education. We trust that the steps and procedures outlined in this guidebook have given you enough information to enable you to successfully maneuver through the difficult and often confusing process of preparing for college.

Beginning with this chapter and continuing through the remainder of this guidebook we will be giving you hints, tips, ideas, mistakes to avoid, phrases you should know, commonly used abbreviations and terms, definitions, and various information sources. The information, which is covered in the next few chapters, should certainly help you polish your college preparation skills and make the task of applying to the colleges and securing financial aid much easier. We suggest that you take the information covered in these final few chapters and incorporate it with the procedures, which we have outlined in the guidebook to this point. By doing this you will be able to take full advantage of this guidebook and achieve your ultimate goal, the best possible college education at the most affordable price.

This chapter covers two basic areas:

1) Facts that you should know regarding financial aid and the financial aid system.

2) Ideas that may help you reduce the amount you spend for your college education.

Facts

The following are facts and occurrences that often happen to students and/or parents when it comes to securing financial aid for college. These are all items that you should be aware and cautious of. They are also items and situations that most colleges and universities hope you are not familiar with.

HOT spot Remember that the more knowledge you have when navigating the college maze, the better off you will be.

Hopefully, by reviewing this chapter and paying close attention to the items covered in it you will be able to put this information to good use and avoid any costly mistakes and/or errors. Please take the time necessary to review, and make notes of, the following facts:

1) Make sure that a college or university who advertises the fact that they will meet 100 percent of the student's need, actually does. (Note—The student's need is the cost of attending college for one year minus the Expected Family Contribution, or EFC.)

Unfortunately, there are a great number of colleges, which advertise that they will meet 100 percent of the need, and they really don't. They actually only meet a portion of the student's need and fill the remainder of the gap with parent loans. Most of these colleges try to keep this information quiet. In fact, the student and parents must actually be looking for this when evaluating the college's award letter (covered in Chapter 14) in order to spot the fact that the colleges are not actually meeting 100 percent of the student's need.

The term *gapping* is used when any college or university does not meet the entire need of the student. For example: If the annual college cost is $24,000 and the Expected Family Contribution is $4,000, this leaves a "need" of $20,000. If the institution then offers the student $17,000 in financial aid, there is a "gap" of $3,000. A number of colleges will then offer a parent loan for the remaining $3,000 and advertise that they have met 100 percent of the student's need, when, in fact, they have not.

In most college directories, which are available at your library or local bookstore, the institutions will commonly advertise what percentage (on average) of the student's need they meet. Obviously, the higher percentage of need that is being met by the college or university, the more financial aid is being awarded. However, you should be very careful and make sure, even though the college is claiming to meet 100 percent of the student's need, when it comes to your financial aid package that they actually are.

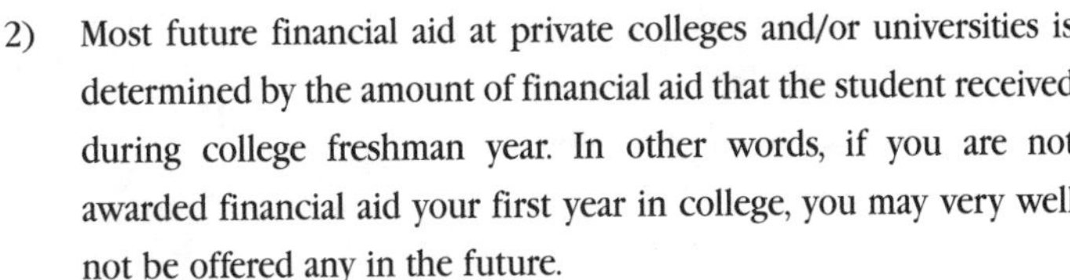

2) Most future financial aid at private colleges and/or universities is determined by the amount of financial aid that the student received during college freshman year. In other words, if you are not awarded financial aid your first year in college, you may very well not be offered any in the future.

It is a fact that with most private colleges first-year financial aid recipients have priority when it comes to reapplication time. The funds that are left over will then be offered to the new applicants. This means that you must do everything possible to make sure you get your fair share of the available financial aid your freshman year. The freshman year financial aid award package literally sets the foundation for all of your future aid. Financial aid is covered in detail in Chapters 10 and 11; in addition, you should take the time necessary to review the procedures which will help you in determining the most lucrative financial aid packages, as covered in Chapters 14 and 15.

3) Upon receiving financial aid from a private source (usually in the form of a scholarship), you should try to determine your college's policy on third-party financial aid. Most colleges, unfortunately, will deduct the amount of your outside scholarship from the financial aid package which they are offering you.

E-Z TIP

The student must notify the institution's financial aid office of the outside award—it is the rules. However, at the same time the student should negotiate to keep both the financial aid awards from the college and the private aid as well. If the college is forced to deduct from the aid package which they offered you, be sure to ask if the amount can be taken from your work-study program or your loan.

Negotiating with the college to prevent it from deducting your outside financial aid award from your gift-aid (or free money) is well worth the time and effort.

4) Certain scholarships and/or financial aid awards are taxable income. It's true. If the student receives outside scholarships that total more than the cost of tuition, fees, books, and supplies, the excess money received is considered taxable income by the Internal Revenue Service.

note

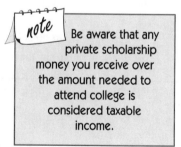

Be aware that any private scholarship money you receive over the amount needed to attend college is considered taxable income.

Although the college's financial aid officer is not obligated to tell you this information, it is the law.

5) The majority of the awarded gift-aid (money that does not have to be worked for, or paid back) commonly goes to in-state residents. In fact, most out-of-state students receive mainly self-help aid (usually work-study jobs and loans) from the college or university.

This is usually the case only as it applies to the institution's financial aid offices. Departmental scholarships from inside the college or university are usually awarded to the students who have shown outstanding achievement, regardless of whether they live in, or out, of the state in which the institution is located.

note

6) If the parents cannot qualify for a Federal PLUS loan because of a poor credit history, the student may be eligible for an additional, unsubsidized Federal Stafford loan with a lower interest rate.

Most financial aid offices will fail to tell you about this particular stipulation; however, it is certainly a viable option because of the help it will offer the student, and the extended grace period between graduation and the time when the loan must be repaid.

7) The importance of meeting all deadlines when applying for any type of financial aid is without question the biggest factor in the entire college preparation process.

Although some financial aid officers, as well as the institutions that they represent, fail to mention the deadlines for the financial aid applications, it is imperative that these deadlines are known ahead of time and met by the student and the parents. These priority deadlines also mean that the college's awarded financial aid is on a first come, first served basis. If these

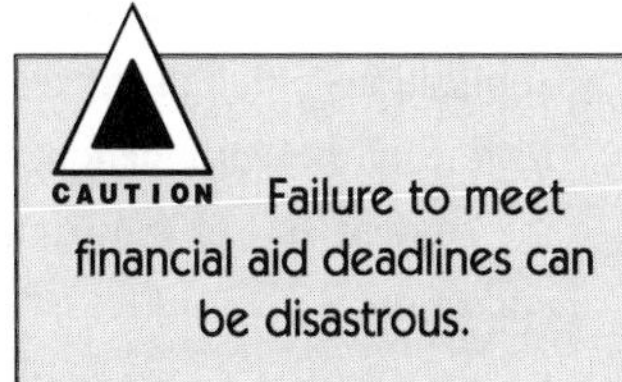
CAUTION Failure to meet financial aid deadlines can be disastrous.

deadlines are missed, the student will be extremely lucky to receive any aid whatsoever.

It is vital to meet all deadlines when applying for financial aid.

8) Although most all financial aid officers do not want to talk about it, or even admit it, they possess the power to alter the student's awarded financial aid by using what is called professional judgement. Professional judgement, as it is used by the college's financial aid officer, can have a great effect on the student's financial aid package.

The financial aid officer reviews the information which is contained in your FAFSA (Free Application for Federal Student Aid) and your CSS/PROFILE application (if applicable) to determine your basic eligibility for financial aid. However, the financial aid officer then has the option of changing the award package as he/she sees fit. This may work either for, or against, the student.

For example, if there have been significant changes in the student's and/or parent's life since the original applications for financial aid were filed, the financial aid officer should be notified immediately. (Note-Details on this are covered in Chapter 15, Negotiating the College's Award Letter.)

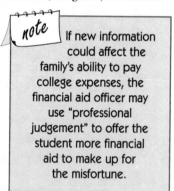

> **note** If new information could affect the family's ability to pay college expenses, the financial aid officer may use "professional judgement" to offer the student more financial aid to make up for the misfortune.

Contrary, the financial aid officer may also review the family's personal information that may not be included on the government's financial aid applications (such as interest income or the value of the student's car). After reviewing this information, the financial aid officer may then determine that the student and/or the family should actually pay more towards the cost of education.

The student and family should be aware of the financial aid officer's ability to use professional judgement when it comes to determining the financial aid package. It is vital that the financial aid officer has current information regarding the financial situation and be informed immediately of any significant changes that could affect their ability to pay college expenses.

9) The student and parents should be very cautious when the college's financial aid office asks for additional information that was not included in the original application(s) for aid. The financial aid office may say that this information is just for their records, or that it is standard procedure, when it is actually information that is used (most of the time) to change the family's EFC (Expected Family Contribution), and ultimately alter the amount the student and family must pay towards the cost of the student's education.

Commonly, some of the questions to be on the lookout for from the college's financial aid office are:

- Will the non-custodial parent pay any of the student's college expenses?
- What are the non-custodial parent's income, assets, and debts?
- What is the equity of the parent's home?
- Will the student drive to school? If so, what is the value of the car the student will be driving?
- How many vehicles do the parents (family) own?
- How much of the student's college expenses do the parents plan to pay for?
- What are the values of the parent's life insurance policies and retirement accounts?

- How much money will the student earn during the summer after graduating from high school?

The institution may very well have internal guidelines that will allow them to adjust the Expected Family Contribution (EFC) based on any additional information that they are able to obtain. Although you may be obligated to answer the questions asked by the college, do not hesitate to ask what the information will be used for. This will help you in targeting your responses to their particular questions.

10) The student will not generally receive any awarded financial aid until after the third week of school. This means that the student will need to have adequate funds to purchase books, supplies, food, housing, and transportation at the beginning of the school year.

After the third or fourth week of college, the financial aid awards will be distributed to the student's accounts. The student will then be reimbursed for the money that was spent at the beginning of the year.

Education

Please remember that the ideas listed below are simply intended to be suggestions. Due to the fact that every student's situation is completely different, a strategy that may work for one student may obviously not be right for the next, and vice versa. You should spend some time reviewing the below listed possible ways to lower your college education costs and hopefully you will be able to locate some tips that apply to your specific situation.

By following the timeline that was outlined in Chapter 2, and putting the procedural strategies outlined in Chapters 3 through 17 to work, the student should be able to effectively navigate the college preparation and funding maze. In addition, by incorporating the hints, tips, ideas, mistakes to avoid, and information sources listed in Chapters 18 through 23, the student will gain additional knowledge that may enable them to reduce their college education expense.

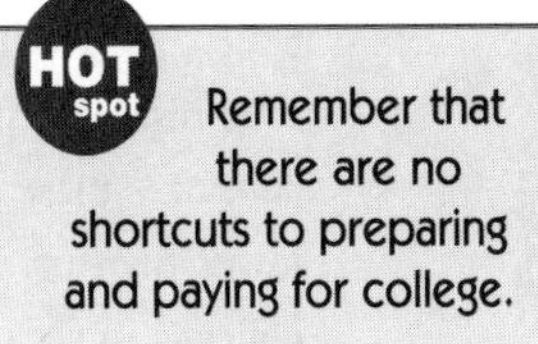

HOT
spot
Remember that there are no shortcuts to preparing and paying for college.

Again, the information listed below is intended to be incorporated into the overall college preparation and funding process that has been outlined previously in this guidebook. It takes time, dedication, and work; however, remember that you are investing in the most important thing of all—your future.

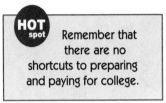

- The National Merit Scholarship Program bases its financial aid awards on the academic merit of the student. These awarded funds may be applied at any college or university to help the student meet the cost of attendance. By taking the PSAT test (covered in Chapter 5) the student will be registered for the National Merit Scholarship Program.

- Most all colleges and universities offer some type of merit (or non-need) based scholarships to those students who are academically talented. The student should check with each institution that they are considering to learn about their available merit scholarships and the application requirements for each.

- Many institutions will offer scholarships to those students who show exceptional athletic talent. The student and/or parents should take the time to weigh the benefits of an athletic scholarship versus the demands involved in accepting this type of awarded financial aid.

- There are some colleges and institutions that offer grants and/or scholarships to students with specific talents in the field of music, journalism, and drama.

- Many states offer financial aid in the form of scholarships to students who are academically talented. If they feel they might qualify, the student may contact their state's office of education to receive eligibility requirements for these particular types of awards.

- State colleges and universities typically charge lower fees to students who reside in the state that the institution is located. State revenues subsidize these public institutions, which makes their tuition costs lower than private schools. When narrowing your list of possible colleges to six finalists (covered in Chapter 6), you should include one of these "safety valve" state colleges into your list. Remember that you should not base your college search and selection process totally on cost. Although the amount the student and/or family pay for the cost of attendance is surely a consideration, it should not be the only one.

- Some colleges and universities offer students special cost of attendance discounts for any, or all, of the following reasons:

    - If more than one student from the same family is enrolled.

    - If the student recruits another student for attendance.

    - If the student is the editor of the college's newspaper or a student government leader.

- Some colleges and universities will convert the student's loans into grants (gift-aid) if the student remains in school and graduates. The student should get the specifics of this benefit, ahead of time, if offered by any of his/her six finalist college selections.

- A few colleges and universities will pay the student's loan origination fee. It is often worth the student's time to inquire if any of his/her six finalist institutions will pay these loan origination fees for him/her.

- There are a great number of colleges and universities that have special funds allotted for students and/or families that do not qualify for federal or state funded financial aid. The student should check with each of him/her six finalist institutions for any additional financial aid that may be available. This additional aid could be vital in making your final college choice selection, as outlined in Chapter 16.

Conclusion

Hopefully some of the ideas outlined in this chapter will help you when preparing and paying for college. Again, these are simply suggestions and should be applied accordingly to each individual student's situation. Remember that the entire college preparation and funding process is a sequential procedure that takes time and a lot of hard work to successfully complete. By having the dedication necessary, and putting forth the necessary effort, the student will ultimately be able to receive the highest quality of education at the most affordable price.

Chapter 19

Mistakes to avoid

What you'll find in this chapter:

- Rumors, myths and frauds
- Missing deadlines
- Don't wait 'til the last minute
- Avoiding financial aid fraud
- Why you must never lie

This chapter goes into great detail regarding the common mistakes made by students and parents when preparing and paying for college. Although these "mistakes" are covered, in detail, throughout this guidebook, we have compiled a list of the most common ones into one convenient source. In addition, we have made reference to the specific chapter(s) that coincide with each potential costly mistake that you may encounter along the way. By double-checking this list and referring to the appropriate chapter you will have a complete understanding of the most common mistakes and how you can avoid them. Most all of these mistakes will cost you time, and practically every one of them will cost you money. It is vital to avoid them at all cost. Take the time necessary to review this chapter and make notes to prevent these mistakes from happening to you.

Hopefully, after reviewing this chapter and making the appropriate notes as they pertain to your particular situation, you will be able to avoid these often-costly mistakes along the way.

This chapter outlines items that you should be aware and cautious of in the college planning and preparation stages. In addition, it also covers ways to avoid being taken advantage of, and what to look for, when it comes to securing financial aid for college. We have divided this chapter into three separate sections:

1) The most common mistakes.

2) Costly errors to avoid.

3) Avoiding costly financial aid frauds.

Common college planning mistakes

We obviously realize that nobody is perfect and that especially holds true when it comes to planning and preparing for college. Hopefully, by reviewing the information listed below, you will be able to avoid some of the common mistakes people make when it comes to the college preparation and funding process. These mistakes usually come in either one of two forms:

1) They are actually myths that someone has heard from a friend or family member and are not actually fact.

2) They are careless errors because some people simply don't want to spend the time and effort necessary to successfully navigate the college preparation and funding process.

Regardless of which way the mistake is made, it can be very costly (both in time and money) to both the student and the parents. In this section we cover both types of mistakes. You should take the time to review these lists (making notes where applicable):

- Assuming that you will not be eligible to receive financial aid for college. Although some financial aid is designed to help the financially needy students and parents, there is also an abundance of aid available for other students with families of all income and asset levels. It is important to remember that students may receive financial aid based on their high school achievements (academics, athletics, or other talents) regardless of their parent's income and/or assets.

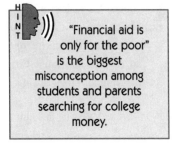

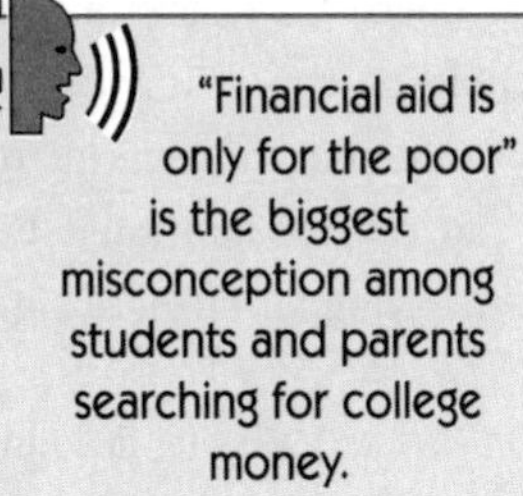

HINT
"Financial aid is only for the poor" is the biggest misconception among students and parents searching for college money.

Most students and families know that some financial aid is available, but they are not actually sure how to locate, apply, and receive this aid. There are several chapters in this guidebook that outline the sources and availability of financial aid, as well as give you detailed instructions on how to effectively apply and receive this aid to help pay for the cost of the student's college education. By using these strategies and with work and dedication, you should be able to locate and secure financial aid money for college.

- During the college search and selection process, removing a college or university from your list of possibilities because you think you would not be able to afford the cost of attendance. This is a very common mistake on the part of a number of high school students who are preparing for college.

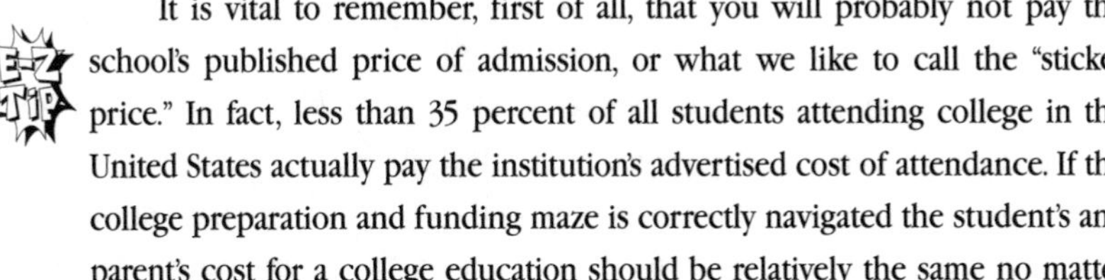

It is vital to remember, first of all, that you will probably not pay the school's published price of admission, or what we like to call the "sticker price." In fact, less than 35 percent of all students attending college in the United States actually pay the institution's advertised cost of attendance. If the college preparation and funding maze is correctly navigated the student's and parent's cost for a college education should be relatively the same no matter which college or university the student attends.

CAUTION

Do not rule out any college because you think you can't afford it. There are dozens of effective methods to obtain the necessary financial aid for college. We realize that paying for college is one of the student's and parent's biggest concerns and we have devoted a great deal of time in this guidebook to help in the securing of financial aid. Financial aid sources and availability are covered in detail in Chapters 8 and 10. In addition, strategies for effectively applying for financial aid are covered in Chapters 9 and 11.

3) Missing deadlines can be disastrous when applying for financial aid, as well as when making admission applications to the colleges and universities. This is a mistake that simply cannot be overcome.

HOT spot

Without question, the most important item to remember regarding the entire college preparation and funding process is: financial aid is always on a first come, first served basis. There are no exceptions to this rule. It is vital to be first in line when applying for financial aid. You should pay close attention to all deadlines and make sure you meet each and every one of them. We have outlined these deadlines in Chapters 2, *Timeline*, 7, *College Admissions Application Process*, 9, *Scholarship Application Process*, and 11, *Financial Aid Application Process*. Remember that missing a deadline will always cost you some financial aid; in fact, by missing a deadline, you may not receive any financial aid at all.

4) Making a college campus visit without first prior arranging the visit. This is a very common mistake; it is something that is taken for granted by thousands of students and parents across the country.

E-Z TIP

It is very important to thoroughly plan your college campus visits and prearrange your itinerary for the entire stay. In addition, the student should make an appointment to meet with both the college's admissions officer and its financial aid officer during the campus visit. The college campus visit is a vital portion of the college selection process and must be given a great deal of attention. Although campus visits require time, and previous planning, they are a must in the college preparation and funding process. Conducting effective campus visits set the foundation for the student's relationship with the institution. Detailed information and ideas for an effective campus visit are covered in Chapter 12.

5) Making application for admission to a college or university that was not first visited by the student and parents. This common mistake is closely related to number 4 above—however, it deserves special note in this chapter due to the serious effect it may have on the student's future.

Although the student may be able to discover several items regarding an institution by reading through brochures, catalogs, or a college directory, it is vital to first visit the institution's campus prior to making application for admission.

Remember that every college is a community and has a personality all its own. The only way for the student to determine if the college community is right for him/her is to visit personally and get a true and accurate feel of what the school has to offer. Again, college campus visits are covered in Chapter 12.

6) Submitting a disorganized, incomplete, or messy application for financial aid and/or college admission acceptance is a definite mistake.

Remember that in most cases the college or university, the scholarship sponsor, and the federal government will determine your eligibility for admission and financial aid based on one basic piece of information: your application. It is vital that these applications be as complete and organized as possible. In addition, taking the time necessary to arrange your applications neatly and professionally will pay great dividends in the long run. Remember that you are making an impression on the persons who are reading your applications. It is vital that this impression be the best it can be.

College admissions applications are covered in Chapter 7, the scholarship application process is covered in Chapter 9, and financial aid applications are covered in Chapter 11.

7) Being dishonest, even slightly, when filling out your college admission applications, your scholarship applications, or your financial aid applications will cost you any chance of acceptance and/or your eligibility for financial aid.

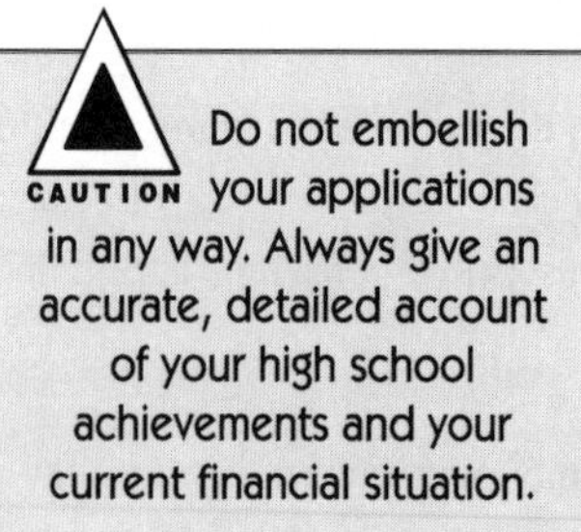

CAUTION
Do not embellish your applications in any way. Always give an accurate, detailed account of your high school achievements and your current financial situation.

Adding items or information beyond your actual situation or accomplishments will cost you dearly in the college preparation and funding process. The financial aid applications are commonly verified (audited) and if a discrepancy is discovered due to your deliberate misinformation contained in the application, you may and/or will lose all available financial aid. In addition, it is important to know and remember that colleges are built on trust and honesty. If the admissions officer who reviews your application discovers that you are not completely truthful, your possibility of being accepted for admittance is virtually zero.

Always be 100 percent honest and accurate on your admissions, scholarship, and financial aid applications.

8) The student's failure to provide letters of recommendation is a far too common mistake. Most all colleges require at least two letters of recommendation (one from your high school counselor and the other from one of your high school teachers) and a large number of institutions commonly ask for several other recommendation letters.

In most cases you will be able to pick the people who write your letters of recommendation. (Exception to this rule is that you generally have very little control over which of your high school guidance counselors will write your recommendation letter.) Remember that the colleges are attempting to discover as much as they can about you, and recommendation letters are a very valuable and often overlooked method of doing this. The letters from your high school teacher(s) and counselor (as well as any other requested sources) are a very important part of the college's admissions officer's decision. Making sure the institutions receive the requested letters of recommendation is a vital portion of the college admission application process. This application process is covered in Chapter 7.

E-Z TIP

It is vital to take the necessary time to secure letters of recommendation from all of the various sources that are listed in Chapter 7. Having these letters ready for the colleges (and also scholarship sponsors) will be a critical part of your application process and will greatly increase your chances of being offered admission (and of receiving financial aid).

9) Letting the parents make the final college choice selection for the student. Parents are certainly advisors; in fact their advice is often very beneficial. However, the student must make the final college selection decision.

We realize that parents want to do nothing more than help their children (student) and genuinely have their best interest in mind. When it comes to making the final college selection, the parents should surely offer advice; but ultimately it must be the student's decision. The student is the one who will spend four years (at least) of his/her life on the campus, not to mention the fact that the student's entire future is also on the line. The parent's suggested roles in the college selection process are covered further in Chapter 12.

HOT spot

Although the student should welcome the parent's advice, the final college selection decision must ultimately be made by the student.

Costly errors to avoid

The following are costly errors that should be avoided by the student and/or the parents during the college preparation and funding process. Although you may now be aware of most (or all) of these mistakes from reading the guidebook to this point, we have arranged a list of the most common critical errors made by students and parents. Take some time and review (making notes where necessary) the below listed information to help you successfully navigate the college preparation and funding maze.

1) Waiting too long before applying for financial aid is an error that is far too common. The most important rule to remember when applying for financial aid is that deadlines are vital and the timeline for applying for financial aid is not based on the college's admission applications deadlines.

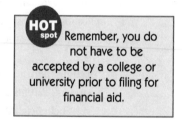

> **HOT spot** Remember, you do not have to be accepted by a college or university prior to filing for financial aid.

note

It is a common myth that students who apply for financial aid first and then to the college will automatically be turned down for admission by the institution. This is simply not the case. Financial aid deadlines, in some cases, come before the student has narrowed his or her list of possible colleges down to six finalists. The financial aid application process and the college admissions application process often overlap each other. Please refer to the timeline that is in Chapter 2 for further details on the most effective time to make your applications for financial aid and for admission. The college admissions application process is also covered in Chapter 7, and the financial aid application process is covered in Chapters 9 and 11.

It is vital to meet all financial aid deadlines (regardless of whether or not the student has applied or been accepted for admittance at a particular institution). This will assure that the application is considered on merit and the student will not lose any available financial aid because of failure to apply on time.

2) Failure to pay the application fee, or spend the money necessary, to complete and submit a CSS/PROFILE financial aid application to any institution that requests it is a mistake made by thousands of students. The CSS/PROFILE financial aid application is similar to the FAFSA (the Free Application for Federal Student Aid, which must be filed by all students who are seeking financial aid); however, the CSS/PROFILE application goes into greater detail regarding specific sections of the family's financial history (such as equity in the family's home, the value of life insurance policies, etc.).

The main point to remember regarding the CSS/PROFILE financial aid application is that usually the institutions that request this application commonly have additional financial aid to give away. These institutions are specific in who receives their awarded financial aid and they require more information than is contained in the FAFSA to make their final decisions. By not taking the time or spending the money (usually around $25 per application) to complete and submit the CSS/PROFILE application, the student greatly reduces his or her chances of receiving the maximum amount of financial aid which is available from that particular institution. Further information on the CSS/PROFILE financial aid application is covered in Chapter 11.

It is very important to spend the time and money necessary to complete and submit the CSS/PROFILE financial aid application to any/all of the institutions that may request it. These institutions are looking for more detailed information in order to distribute their additional financial aid to the most qualified applicants.

The CSS/PROFILE does not take the place of the FAFSA. It is a separate financial aid form that is often requested in addition to the FAFSA. All students who are applying for any type of financial aid must fill out and submit the Free

Application for Federal Student Aid (FAFSA) with the federal government regardless of what other applications may be requested.

3) The misunderstanding and/or failure to correct your Student Aid Report (SAR) can be devastating when it comes to being awarded financial aid. This is such an important part of the financial aid process; we have broken this information into two different categories (misunderstanding the Student Aid Report and the correcting of your Student Aid Report). This will hopefully give you a better understanding of each specific area.

- Misunderstanding the Student Aid Report. The SAR has several different sections and contains several different types of possible financial aid awards. Do not mistake the terminology that may deny you one particular type of financial aid to mean that you are being totally denied any financial aid whatsoever. For example: the SAR will commonly say that based on your submitted information you are not eligible for a Federal Pell Grant. This simply means that you are not eligible for a Pell Grant; however, there are several other forms of financial aid for which you may qualify.

Don't take this wording to mean a turndown for all other available types of financial aid.

- Correcting your Student Aid Report is vital. There are dozens of items contained in your SAR (your current financial situation, your Social Security number, your finalist college selections, etc.) that should be double-checked for accuracy. Failure to make the necessary corrections and immediately resubmit your updated version of your SAR could be disastrous when it comes to receiving financial aid for college.

Taking the time necessary to review and update (if necessary) your Student Aid Report is an extremely important step in the financial aid process.

Further details on the Student Aid Report are covered in Chapter 11, Financial Aid Application Process.

4) Not immediately accepting all of the college's admission offers is a vital error on the part of the student. Accepting all offers (both for admission and financial aid) are extremely vital steps in the college preparation and funding process.

By accepting all offers you will be reserving the awarded financial aid in your name. We realize that you will eventually be selecting one final college. At that time you will be able to go back and notify the non-selected colleges that you are relinquishing both your admission offers and your awarded financial aid with that particular institution. These procedures are covered in Chapters 13, 14, 15, and 16.

It is vital to first accept all financial aid offers as well as offers for admission and then later (after you have sorted through your possibilities and made your final decision) to relinquish the offers at the schools you reject. Remember that you have spent the time and energy necessary to effectively apply for admission and financial aid and have met all the important deadlines. Now be sure to take advantage of all your efforts by first accepting any/all offers made to you and then evaluating each offer to make your final determination.

5) Verification of your financial aid eligibility by the college is a common practice and must be taken seriously by the student and parents. Commonly, 30 percent of students who receive financial aid are verified. This verification procedure is a federal regulation and must be done.

You may receive a standard verification form from the college that will ask for any or all of the following information:

- Identify all members of the student's household.

- ✧ Disclose any untaxed income.

- ✧ A copy of the student's and parent's federal tax forms and applicable W-2 forms.

It is important to remember that the verification process is designed to provide quality control for the financial aid system. Verification cannot be prevented, and in order to receive your awarded financial aid, you must reply promptly in the event that you are verified. There are certain colleges and universities which commonly verify every applicant (student) as part of the standard financial aid procedure. This verification procedure may catch any mistakes that you made when originally applying for financial aid and by making the necessary corrections, you may be eligible for additional financial aid. Verification, in some instances, can actually work to the advantage of the student and the parents.

It is vital to respond to a verification request quickly and accurately. Failure to do so will cancel any federal financial aid that you may have been scheduled to receive.

6) Failing to reapply for financial aid is a mistake no student can afford to make.

This guidebook has covered how the student's high school years set the foundation for the college career, including all financial aid. By the time you are a college freshman, you have spent years preparing yourself and countless hours researching and making the necessary applications, etc. in order to receive the highest quality of education at the most affordable price. Unlike admissions, financial aid is not automatically renewed each year. Financial aid is an annual event and must be reapplied for as such. This financial aid renewal application process is covered in Chapter 17.

It is vital that during your college freshman year you reapply for financial aid for the upcoming year, your sophomore year. The federal government will mail renewal FAFSA (Free Application for Federal Student Aid) applications

directly to the students who are currently receiving financial aid, usually in November or December of the freshman year. Due to the fact that these renewal FAFSA applications can often get lost or misplaced, you should be aware of the fact that you must reapply for financial aid each and every year, regardless if you receive your renewal FAFSA or not. The institution's financial aid office should have a renewal FAFSA financial aid form, or you may obtain one at the government's web-site, which is located at *www.fafsa.ed.gov*

Avoiding costly financial aid frauds

The first two sections of this chapter covered common errors and mistakes that often prove costly to high school students searching for financial aid. In this section we will go over common financial aid frauds that may cost the student and/or the family money through no fault of their own. These offers often seem very good to start with; however, the companies offering them usually fall short of their claims. The Federal Trade Commission estimates that a minimum of 10,000 questionable financial aid search services defraud over 300,000 high school students (and their families) out of millions of dollars each year. It is important to note that there are also reputable college financial aid search services available.

In order to protect themselves, the student and family must be very cautious and investigate the companies completely before they enroll with any service.

Sometimes financial aid frauds can be very hard to spot. The students and families must be aware of the following tactics that are commonly used by fraudulent companies:

- Do not think you are above being scammed. Anyone is susceptible to financial aid scams and everyone should be aware of the fact that this possibility does exist.

The financial aid scam companies know the confusion that the students and parents face when preparing for college and they often take advantage of this uncertainty. In addition, these financial aid scam companies also know of the desperation that is often felt by the high school student and their family when it comes to college expenses.

Remember to always be on the lookout—anyone can be a victim of these financial aid scam companies.

- Be aware of the common terminology often used by the financial aid scam companies:
    - I can get anyone financial aid.
    - You can't get this valuable information anywhere else.
    - You must act now, before the money is gone. (It is true that deadlines are a very important part of the financial aid process; however, financial aid scam companies use this to their advantage. Be careful.)
    - All you need to do is give me all of your information and we will do all of the work for you.
    - There are countless millions of dollars in financial aid that goes unclaimed every year. (This is somewhat true; however, these awards are usually for specific groups of students—children whose parent works for a specific corporation, etc.—and you would commonly not be eligible for these awards in the first place.)
    - Your bank account number and your credit card will reserve this award in your student's name.

All of these are common terms and the language often used by financial aid scam companies. Be wary of these when considering any company.

- If the financial aid or scholarship search company requests that you pay a deposit or application fee in order to receive the scholarship award, be very cautious. This is most always a sign of a scam and should be avoided by students and parents. These companies may also ask for credit card and/or bank account information.

- Paying for free information is a common mistake students and parents make when searching for scholarships. Many companies will charge students for access to scholarship data bases that are commonly accessible for free over the Internet. Chapter 8, Scholarship Sources and Types, and Chapter 23, Information Sources, both contain web-sites that offer free scholarship search services.

Paying for a scholarship search service when the information is usually obtained for free is definitely a scam and should be avoided.

- When a company "guarantees" that you will receive a scholarship award or you will get your money back this is almost always a scam. There is no third party that can guarantee another company's (scholarship sponsors) money to begin with.

These companies commonly provide the student with a list of scholarship sponsors (which the students may have obtained for free by themselves) to which the student must apply. Some of the guarantees make the claim that they will refund the money paid for their service if every prospective scholarship sponsor on the list turns down the student. Unfortunately, it is very unlikely that the student will hear from every scholarship sponsor to which they applied. Consequently, the student will then not be able to prove being turned down by each sponsor and will not get the "guaranteed" refund promised.

- Some scholarship scam companies disguise themselves as contests in order to attract students in search of financial aid. .

- Use 800 toll-free numbers; however, be aware of any 900 numbers that have a standard per-minute charge involved. You should also be cautious of an 800 toll-free number that forwards the caller to a 900 number with a fee involved.

CAUTION
Be wary of any contest that offers a college scholarship as the prize.

HINT

These 900 numbers are expensive and you spend most of your time listening to the promises of the scam-company with no actual results and/or benefits to the student.

Even if a company has a toll-free 800 number, it is no sign that the company is legitimate. It is fast and easy to set up a toll-free number today and can be done by practically anyone. Be on the lookout for any and all 800 and 900 numbers you may be attempting to do business with.

Below is a list of common "red flags" that you should be aware of when it comes to financial aid companies:

- An official sounding name or fancy logo is almost always a sign that the company is a scam. Words such as "national," "official," and "federation" are all signs of a financial aid scam company.

- A post office box on the company's letterhead or in their brochures, etc. is also a sign of a scam.

- If you are offered an easy, or guaranteed, acceptance it is probably a financial aid scam.

Remember that the financial aid process is hard work and takes many hours to successfully complete. Any promises you receive stating that the process is easy, or that they will do all the work for you is almost always a scam.

If you have further questions regarding financial aid scams, or you would like to inquire further concerning a particular company, you may do so by contacting one of the following groups:

National Fraud Information Center
P.O. Box 65868
Washington, DC 20035
Telephone: (800) 876-7060 or (202) 835-0159
Fax: (202) 835-0767
E-mail: *nfic@internetmci.com*

Council of Better Business Bureaus
4200 Wilson Blvd., Suite 800
Arlington, VA 22203
Telephone: (703) 276-0100 or (703) 525-8277
E-mail: *bbb@bbb.org*

Federal Trade Commission "Scholar Scam"
P.O. Box 99-6
Washington, DC 20050
E-mail: *consumerline@FTC.gov*

Chapter 20

Phrases you should know

What you'll find in this chapter:

- Understanding the college scoring system
- Knowing "special applications"
- Building a freshman class
- Useful terms and acronyms

This chapter covers the phrases that are commonly used by college officials. Although the terms outlined in this chapter are not actually a secret, the college officials will try their best not to use any of these phrases around students and/or their parents.

These phrases make up the workings of the college admission and financial aid system as seen through the eyes of the college officials. This chapter is intended to familiarize you with these terms so that you may become further aware of the procedures the colleges use in accepting a student, as well as determining a financial aid package. Remember that the more knowledge you have about the workings of the college preparation and funding process, the better decision you will be able to make. By reading through this chapter and making notes on the important items, you will no doubt have gained additional information that may help you in the college preparation and funding process.

Application score

All colleges, whether they want to admit it or not, use some type of scoring system to rate their applicants. Colleges and universities receive literally thousands of admission applications and they must have a way of keeping track of each individual applicant.

There are several different rating systems used by the institutions. They may assign numbers, letters, etc. to each application they receive. It is not important to the student what type of scoring systems are used by the colleges; it is only important to know that these rating systems do exist.

Commonly, each portion of the student's admission application is assigned a score and then the application is given an over-all rating. This rating will ultimately decide the student's future at that particular institution.

Here are the common areas of the student's admission application that are usually given a score by the institution:

- Grade point average. This average is usually not the one that was determined by the student's high school; instead, this average is usually determined by using the college's formula that is based on the difficulty of the classes taken by the student in high school and the grades received in each class. This will give the institution an accurate grade point average for all of its applicants.

- SAT and/or ACT scores. The importance of SAT and ACT testing, along with ideas and procedures necessary to test effectively, are covered in Chapter 5.

- Activities the student participated in while in high school. (Remember, colleges are looking for active participants, not students who join several clubs and organizations but fail to be active in any of them.)

- Recommendation letters from the student's high school counselor and teachers. (Some institutions may request more than these two recommendation letters. It is definitely to the student's advantage to include as many letters of recommendation as possible in the college admission application packet.)

- The student's essay. The essay is usually given two separate scores, one for the student's writing ability and the other for the content of the essay. Hints, tips, and ideas for writing an effective essay are covered in Chapter 7.

Several institutions now assign two admissions officers to each applicant. Each officer will then review the student's application and each will assign a score. Generally, if your average score of each admissions officer is over a certain level you will automatically be offered admission; likewise, if your score is below a certain criteria, you will be declined. Most students usually fall somewhere in between the high and the low criteria and their applications are then referred to the admissions committee for the final decision.

Further details on how to arrange and complete a powerful and effective college admissions application are covered in Chapter 7.

Admit-deny

This term is used a great deal by the college's admissions officer, as well as the institution's financial aid officer.

DEFINITION

To understand what *admit-deny* means, you must first understand the process the colleges go through in order to enroll its new freshmen every year. The college knows how many new freshmen they are going to require each year to keep the classes full and everyone happy. In addition, the college also knows how many students they will have to offer admission in order to get their allotted number of new freshmen. For example: if the college needs 800 new freshman, they will generally accept 2,400 applicants because they know that only one out of every three that is accepted actually enrolls and attends. After the 2,400 applicants are offered admission the term admit-deny comes into play.

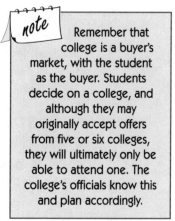

> *note*
>
> Remember that college is a buyer's market, with the student as the buyer. Students decide on a college, and although they may originally accept offers from five or six colleges, they will ultimately only be able to attend one. The college's officials know this and plan accordingly.

Out of these 2,400 students, there are 800 or so that they are very anxious to enroll, 800 that are in the middle, and 800 that are towards the bottom of the list. This means that the college will then offer the top 800 the most lucrative financial aid packages to encourage them to become part of the institution's new freshman class. (This goes back to the old saying the most attractive students will receive the most lucrative financial aid "offers." It is vital to make your application stand out, to make your achievements shine for the colleges. This could literally make thousands of dollars worth of difference in the financial aid package you are offered.)

Contrarily, the college will offer the bottom 800 applicants a very limited financial aid package. Although some of these students may be able to attend this particular college without the help of any financial aid, most of them can't. If these bottom 800 accepted students have been offered admission, but have not been offered enough financial aid to make their enrollment possible, then they fall under the term "admit-deny."

Flag

DEFINITION

A *flag* is a distinguishing mark on an admission application that denotes the application is special. There are three common groups of applicants who receive a flag:

1) Students who have special talents.

2) Students of alumni.

3) Students who are a part of an under-represented minority.

If an admission application is "flagged" then it is moved from the large group of all other applicants and considered separately.

Need-based admission

Although most colleges will not admit it, they often take the student's and parent's assets (wealth) into consideration when determining the student's eligibility for enrollment. This ability to pay does not figure into the scenario at the beginning of the college's selection process; only as the financial aid at the institution begins to run out. (This again stresses the importance of being first in line with your applications for financial aid.)

Although this term is called "need-based admission" it is actually need-based denial. If the institution's financial aid resources are practically depleted and a questionable student has a financial need, they are often overlooked (denied admission) for a student with a lesser financial need and more ability to pay the cost of attendance themselves.

Building a freshman class

Maintaining an equal balance of racial, ethnic, geographic, and economic diversity is important to most colleges and universities around the country. In order to achieve this diversity, the institution "builds a freshman class," with the opportunity to offer admission to the students who fill the gaps they need in order to have a diversified campus. (The college may also take gender-balance into consideration when determining who is offered admission.)

Preferential packaging

Preferential packaging simply means that the most attractive students will receive the most lucrative financial aid offers. These more attractive financial aid offers could have a variety of advantages for the student, ranging from a better division of gift-aid and self-help aid to a discount off the institution's advertised cost of attendance (sticker price).

Hopefully the phrases listed above will give you a better feel for the terminology used by the college's admissions officers and financial aid officers. Remember that the better knowledge you have of the system, the better you will be able to navigate the college preparation and funding maze.

Chapter 21

Common abbreviations

The terminology used by the institutions and the federal government to describe the college preparation and funding process have become so complicated and confusing most people have no idea what these items mean. To help you better understand the process, we have included a list of the most commonly used abbreviations below. This will hopefully give you a clearer picture of the language, abbreviations, and terms that are being used.

A brief definition is listed beside each abbreviation, with more detailed explanations beside those that will likely be of the most importance to you.

ACT—American College Test—The ACT is one of the two major college entrance exams that are given nationally. This test is conducted through the American College Testing Program. This exam tests the student's knowledge in specific subjects and then combines each individual subject score into a composite score. The highest, or perfect, score on the ACT is a 36. The national average is around 19 or 20. All colleges require that a prospective student applicant take either the ACT or its competitor, the SAT; in fact, most institutions will accept either one.

ADC—Aid to Dependent Children

AFDC—Aid to Families with Dependent Children

AGI—Adjusted Gross Income

AY—Academic Year

BA—Bachelor's Degree

BIA—Bureau of Indian Affairs

COA—Cost of Attendance

CPS—Central Processing System

CSS—College Scholarship Service—is a division of a company called The College Board. College Scholarship Service's primary purpose is to administer the CSS/PROFILE financial aid application for those colleges and universities which require more detailed information regarding the student and the parents prior to making their determination of the student's financial aid eligibility. (If one of your college finalists selections requests a CSS/PROFILE application, you will need to contact CSS and request one. The CSS/PROFILE application has a fee—usually around $20. The student simply cannot afford to overlook the CSS/PROFILE application. The rewards for paying the application fee and spending the necessary time to give the institution further information about the families financial condition will most always pay dividends in the form of additional financial aid for college.)

DHHS—Department of Health and Human Services

ED—United States Department of Education

EDE—Electronic Data Exchange

EFA—Estimated Financial Assistance

EFC—Expected Family Contribution—this is the amount that the student and family are expected to pay towards the student's annual cost of education. The federal government determines your EFC. They use a formula to calculate your "share" based on the figures that were submitted by you and your family on your Free Application for Federal Student Aid (FAFSA). (This EFC is the same no matter which institution you may choose. That means that your actual cost of attendance should be relatively the same no matter which school you pick.) Your financial "need" is then determined by subtracting your EFC from the institution's actual cost of attendance for one year. This "need" is the amount of money that you will hopefully be securing enough financial aid to cover.

EFN—Exceptional Financial Need

EIC—Earned Income Credit

ETS—Educational Testing Service—is the company that prepares, administers, and scores the SAT (Scholastic Aptitude Test). The SAT is the other (besides the ACT) major college entrance exam that is required by the colleges and given nationally.

FAA—Financial Aid Administrator—Financial Aid Director—Financial Aid Officer—the institution's designated official who reviews and processes financial aid applications and determines to what degree the student's financial need will be met by awarding a combination of grants, loans, and/or work-study. He or she is also a manager or administrator who interprets and implements federal, state, and institutional policies and regulations, and may also make necessary changes in the student's financial aid package by using professional judgement.

FADHPS—Financial Assistance for Disadvantaged Health Professions Students

FAFSA—Free Application for Federal Student Aid—is a form that must be submitted by every student who is seeking financial aid. The FAFSA kick-starts the entire financial aid process.

FAT—Financial Aid Transcript

FDLP—Federal Direct Loan Program

FFELP—Federal Family Education Loan Program—pays loans for the cost of college that come directly from banks. The other types of student loans, direct loans, come from the colleges themselves. The student's loan origination point is of no consequence; the amount of money received by the student and the loan repayment terms are not affected either way.

FM—Federal Methodology

FNAS—Federal Need Analysis System

FPLUS—Federal PLUS (Parent) Loan

FSEOG—Federal Supplemental Educational Opportunity Grant

FWS—Federal Work-Study—is a program designed to offer the eligible students campus-based jobs to earn extra money to pay for the cost of their education. The federal government disburses to the institutions funds that cover 75 percent of the student's wages. Students who participate in the FWS program will be paid by the hour and receive at least minimum wage. Only students who demonstrate financial need are eligible for the Federal Work-Study program.

GPA—Grade Point Average

GRE—Graduate Record Examination—this is the required entrance exam for students who are entering graduate school.

GSL—Guaranteed Student Loan

HEAL—Health Education Assistance Loan

HHS—Department of Health and Human Services (also abbreviated DHHS)

HPSL—Health Professions Student Loan Program—a long term, low interest loan program designed to assist students in specific health profession disciplines.

INS—Immigration and Naturalization Service

IPA—Income Protection Allowance

IRS—Internal Revenue Service

ISIR—Institutional Student Information Record—is the report received by the colleges from the government, which contains the determination of your eligibility for federal financial aid based on your FAFSA application. (The student receives the same information in the form of a Student Aid Report—or SAR.)

LDS—Loans for Disadvantaged Students (health professions)

MDE—Multiple Data Entry

NDSL—National Defense/Direct Student Loan (now known as the Federal Perkins Loan)

NEISP—National Early Intervention Scholarship and Partnership Program

NHSC—National Health Service Corps

NSL—Nursing Student Loan

NSLDS—National Student Loan Data System

NSSP—National Science Scholars Program

OSFAP—Office of Student Financial Assistance Programs, United States

PC—Parental Contribution—the amount that the federal government expects the parents to contribute annually towards the cost of the student's college education. This amount is arrived at through information that was submitted by the student and the family in the Free Application for Federal Student Aid form (FAFSA).

PCL—Primary Care Loan Program

PLUS—Parent Loans for Undergraduate Students—are designed for parents to be able to borrow some or all of the Expected Family Contribution. These loans are available only to the parents and provide them with a way of filling the gap in any financial aid package that does not cover the student's financial need.

SAP—Satisfactory Academic Program

SAR—Student Aid Report—is received by the student and family and outlines the federal government's findings and determination of financial aid eligibility based on the information that was submitted in the FAFSA. In addition, the SAR will also contain a list of the institutions that will receive your information in the form of an ISIR. These colleges use the information contained in the ISIR to help them determine the amount of financial aid they will offer you.

SAT—Scholastic Aptitude Testing—is the best known admission exam required by the colleges and universities across the United States. This test is designed to measure the student's aptitude to perform college work and is given to over one million students per year. A perfect score on the SAT is 1600. The lowest possible score is 400, and the national average is around 900. In addition to the original SAT, they now offer 17 separate tests over a variety of different subjects to help the institutions further determine the student's ability to successfully complete the required college courses.

SC—Student Contribution—the amount that the federal government expects the student to contribute annually towards the cost of his/her college education. This amount is arrived at through information that was submitted by the student and the family in the Free Application for Federal Student Aid form (FAFSA).

SDS—Scholarships for Disadvantaged Students

SEOG—Supplemental Educational Opportunity Grant—federal grants for students with exceptional financial need.

SSIG—State Student Incentive Grant

VA—Department of Veterans Affairs

Resources

Where you'll find these Resources:

••• Online Resources •••

- **The Ambitious Student's Guide to Financial Aid**

  www.signet.com/collegemoney/tocl.html

  This is an online book, which includes many worksheets, graphs, and tables; in addition, it offers advice on how to obtain financial aid for college.

- **Chinook College Funding Service**

  www.chinook.com

  This site contains a wide variety of information regarding the financial aid process, and financial aid sources. Chinook is a nationally noted, award winning search service, with an excellent reputation in the field of college preparation and funding.

- **Chronicle of Higher Education**

  www.chronicle.merit.edu

  This site offers a good reference source to keep the student and family up with the ongoing changes in the financial aid process.

- **College Board Online**

  www.collegeboard.org

  This site offers information regarding colleges, their admission requirements, entrance exams, and similar related topics.

- **CollegeEdge**

  www.CollegeEdge.com

  CollegeEdge offers a scholarship search service with a database of over 3,000 institutions and over 3,500 different scholarship sponsors. This site also allows you to investigate many different colleges and universities, finding information that ranges from the cost of attendance to facts and statistics regarding each particular institution.

- **College Funding Solutions, Inc.**
  www.CFSolutions.org
  This site offers the student and the parents help and guidance in navigating the very complex and often confusing college preparation and funding maze. College Funding Solutions, Inc. guides the student and the family through the entire college selection, preparation, and funding process; making sure all deadlines are met, and all forms are completed.
- **CollegeNet**
  www.collegenet.com
  The CollegeNet offers an extensive college database that enables the student to conduct an online search of institutions across the country. This site also offers links to the various colleges and universities.
- **College Xpress**
  www.collegexpress.com/index.html
  This site offers information on colleges and universities including admission requirements, and financial aid information.
- **CollegeSelect**
  www.cyber-u.com
  CollegeSelect offers registration information for four-year colleges and universities in the United States.
- **Department of Education, Office of Post-Secondary Education**
  www.ed.gov/offices/OPE/Students
  This site, sponsored by the federal government, offers the student and parents a variety of information regarding all types of financial aid.
- **Ecola Directories College Locator**
  www.ecola.com/college
  Ecola contains more than 2,500 links to colleges and universities across the country, including their libraries and alumni pages.
- **ExPan Scholarship Search**
  www.collegeboard.org/fundfinder/bin/fundfind01.p1
  ExPan offers an online database for locating scholarship sponsors and funds. The student enters information regarding him or herself and the "free" online search will return any scholarships that may be available to them based on the information that was entered. There are thousands of potential scholarships listed in this database.
- **FAFSA Express**
  www.ed.gov/offices/OPE/express.html
  This site allows the student to download, complete, and electronically submit the Free Application for Federal Student Aid (FAFSA). The site will provide you with a signature sheet, which you must sign and forward to the Processing Center before your FAFSA can be processed.
- **FastAid**
  www.fastaid.com/scholarships/steps.htm
  This site offers an extensive scholarship database, which may be used by the student to locate additional financial aid sources.

- **fastWEB**

  www.fastweb.com

  fastWEB offers an enormous database of scholarships, fellowships, grants, and loans. The student enters all pertinent information regarding themselves and their personal accomplishments and this "free" scholarship search service will return the list of scholarships for which the student may be eligible. In addition, the student has the option of setting up a personalized mailbox in order to receive additional possible award sponsors, as they become available.

- **FinAid – The Financial Aid Information Page**

  www.finaid.com

  This site offers a variety of information regarding financial aid, ranging from financial aid calculators to laws and lenders. This site also offers listings of specialized scholarships.

- **KapLoan**

  www.kaploan.com

  Kaploan offers a well-organized information source for students and parents regarding educational student loans. Through this site, the student and family also have the ability to calculate their Expected Family Contribution (EFC).

- **MOLIS Scholarship Search**

  www.fie.com/molis/scholar.htm

  This site is designed specifically to help minority groups locate and obtain scholarship money for college. It bases its scholarship search service on race, gender, age, and location.

- **NACAC – National Association of College Admissions Counselors**

  www.nacac.com

  This site provides very useful information for the student and parents, offering a behind-the-scenes look into the financial aid issues and new developments in the field.

- **Peterson's Education Center**

  www.petersons.com/resources/finance.html

  Peterson's offers extensive financial aid information for both the student and the parents, and is considered one of the top sites on the web regarding financial aid.

- **The Princeton Review**

  www.review.com/College/Find/index.html

  This site offers an extensive tutorial on the many types of student loans and how to obtain them.

- **Sallie Mae**

  www.slma.com/xalternate.html

  This site offers an extensive look at the ins and outs of student loans, including information on the lenders and their repayment terms.

- **Scholarship Resource Network TM., Daigle and Vierra, Inc.**

  www.rams.com/srn

  This site offers a "free" scholarship search service.

- **Student Services**
  www.studentservices.com/search
  Student Services offers an extensive, searchable database of more than 180,000 financial aid sources. These available scholarships are mainly in the private sector. This site does require on-site registration.

- **The Student Guide**
  www.ed.gov/prog_info/SFA/StudentGuide/1999-2000
  This is a yearly service that is provided by the United States Department of Education and describes for the student and parents information on deadlines, grants, and loans.

- **United States Department of Education**
  www.ed.gov/offices/OPE/Students/index.html
  This site is provided and maintained by the United States government and offers a full-range of information on all types of financial aid for college.

- **U.S. News.Edu**
  www.usnews.com/usnews/edu
  This U.S. News and World Report site gives the student and parents the latest information regarding colleges and universities and how they rank among all of the other institutions in the country. This will help give the student and parents some additional insight when making choices regarding the college selection process.

••• Software •••

- **Apply Technology**
  www.weapply.com
  Software, links, and electronic applications to hundreds of colleges and universities.

- **ExPan – The College Board**
  (800) 223-9726
  This software offers a searchable database with more than 3,000 colleges listed. ExPan is not usually a product for home use; however, it is available at many high schools and libraries across the country.

- **John Hancock Financial Aid Software**
  (800) 633-1809
  This software allows the student and parents to estimate the future tuition, room, and board at over 1,500 public and private institutions.

- **KapLoan Financial Contribution Estimator**
  www.kaploan.com/software.html
  This handy software helps the student and family estimate their contribution to the student's educational cost by figuring the Expected Family Contribution (EFC).

••• Important Phone Numbers •••

Information hotlines

- Free Application for Federal Student Aid (FAFSA) Information Center (319) 337-5665
- FAFSA Express Questions (800) 801-0576
- Federal Student Aid Information Center - Federal Student Aid Hotline (800) 433-3243
- College Scholarship Service - CSS (609) 771-7725
- Financial Aid CSS/PROFILE Application Questions (800) 778-6888
- FastWEB (800) 327-8932
- College Board (212) 713-8000
- Kaplan Student Loan Information Program (888) 527-5626
- National and Community Service Program - AmeriCorps (800) 942-2677
- Selective Service (847) 688-6888
- Social Security Administration (800) 772-1213
- College Answer Service - Sallie Mae (800) 222-7182 or (800) 239-4211
- College Savings Bank (800) 888-2723

Direct loans

(These loans are serviced by the United States Department of Education.)

- Direct Loan Origination Center - Applicant Services (800) 557-7394
- Direct Loan Origination Center - Loan Consolidation (800) 557-7392
- Direct Loan Servicing Center (800) 848-0979
- Direct Loan Servicing Center Consolidation Department (800) 848-0982
- Direct Loan Servicing Center - Office of Collections (800) 848-0981
- Direct Loan Servicing Center - Debt Collection Service (800) 621-3115
- Direct Loan School Relations - Origination and Servicing (800) 848-0978

••• Loan Programs •••

(Banks and institutions that offer various student loan programs.)

- Access Group (800) 282-1550
- American Express College Loan Program (800) 814-4595
- Bank of America (800) 344-8382
- Bank of Boston (800) 226-7866

- Bank One Educational Finance Group (800) 487-4404
- Chase Manhattan Bank (800) 242-7339
- Citibank Student Loans Corporation (800) 692-8200
- Commerce Bank (800) 666-3910
- First Union Educational Loan Services (800) 995-8805
- Fleet Education Finance (800) 235-3385
- GATE Student Loan Program (800) 895-4283
- Independent Federal Savings Bank (800) 733-0473
- KeyBank USA (800) 539-5363
- Mellon Bank EduCheck (800) 366-7011
- Nellie Mae - Excel and Share Loans (800) 634-9308
- Sallie Mae - College Answer Service (800) 239-4211
- Signet Bank Educational Funding (800) 434-1988
- United Student Aid Funds (800) 635-3785

Loan processing centers

(These agencies clear the loans for disbursements and may also provide information regarding your loan application.)

- American Student Assistance (800) 999-9080
- New York State Higher Education Services Corporation (800) 642-6234
- Pennsylvania Higher Education Assistance Authority (800) 692-7392
- Texas Student Loan Corporation (800) 845-6267
- United Student Aid Funds (800) 824-7044

Loan consolidation

(These agencies allow for loan consolidation into one monthly payment.)

- Nellie Mae (800) 634-9308
- Pennsylvania Higher Education Assistance Agency (800) 692-7392
- Sallie Mae (800) 524-9100

Loan forgiveness program

(Note- Information regarding the forgiveness of student loans.)

- The National College Scholarship Foundation (301) 548-9423

Tuition payment plans

(Note- These organizations offer tuition payment plans.)

- Academic Management Service (800) 635-0120
- EduServ Tuition Installment Plan (800) 445-4236
- FACTS Tuition Management System (800) 624-7092
- Key Education Resources (800) 225-6783
- Tuition Management Systems, Inc. (800) 722-4867

••• State Prepaid Tuition Plans •••

(These states have prepaid tuition plans available.)

- Alabama (800) 252-7228
- Alaska (907) 474-7469
- Colorado (800) 478-5651
- Florida (800) 552-4723
- Indiana (317) 232-6386
- Kentucky (800) 928-8926
- Louisiana (800) 259-5626 extension 1012
- Massachusetts (800) 449-6332 option 1
- Maryland (800) 903-7875
- Michigan (800) 243-2847
- Mississippi (800) 987-4450
- Ohio (800) 589-6882 or (800) 233-6734
- Pennsylvania (800) 440-4000
- Tennessee (888) 486-2378
- Texas (800) 445-4723
- Virginia (888) 567-0540
- Wisconsin (888) 338-3789

••• Miscellaneous•••

- Academic Common Market (410) 974-2750
- Council of Better Business Bureaus (703) 276-0100
- Institute of International Education (212) 883-8200
- Americorps National and Community Service Program (800) 942-2677
- USA Group (800) 562-6872
- United States Department of Education, Inspector General Hotline (800) 647-8733
- Western Interstate Commission for Higher Education (303) 541-0210

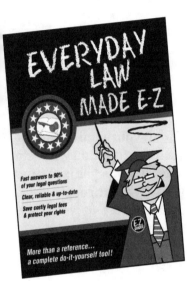

Whatever you need to know we've made it E-Z!

Informative text and forms you can fill ou on-screen.* From personal to business, lega to leisure—we've made it E-Z!

PERSONAL & FAMILY

For all your family's needs, we have titles that will help keep you organized and guide you through most every aspect of your personal life.

BUSINESS

Whether you're starting from scratch with a home business or you just want to keep your corporate records in shape, we've got the programs for you.

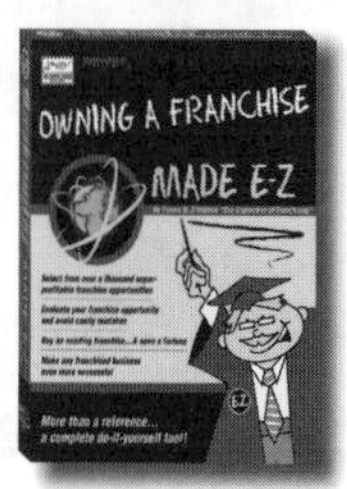

* Not all topics include forms

ss 1999.r2

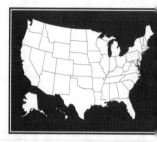

By the book...

MADE E-Z BOOKS provide all the forms you need to take care of business and save on legal fees – *only $29.95 each!*

Everyday Legal Forms & Agreements Made E-Z *ISBN 1-56382-301-2*
A do-it-yourself legal library of 301 ready-to-use perforated legal documents for virtually every personal or business need!

Corporate Record Keeping Made E-Z *ISBN 1-56382-304-7*
Keep your own corporate records current and in compliance... without a lawyer!

Managing Employees Made E-Z *ISBN 1-56382-302-0*
Over 240 documents to manage your employees more efficiently and legally!

Vital Record Keeping Made E-Z *ISBN 1-56382-300-4*
201 simple and ready-to-use forms to help you keep organized records for your family, your business and yourself!

Collecting Unpaid Bills Made E-Z *ISBN 1-56382-309-8*
Essential for anyone who extends credit and needs an efficient way to collect.

Available at:

Super Stores, Office Supply Stores, Drug Stores, Hardware Stores, Bookstores, and other fine retailers.

ss 1999.r2

	Item#	Qty.	Price Ea.‡
E✦Z Legal Kits			
Bankruptcy	K100		$23.95
Incorporation	K101		$23.95
Divorce	K102		$29.95
Credit Repair	K103		$21.95
Living Trust	K105		$21.95
Living Will	K106		$23.95
Last Will & Testament	K107		$18.95
Buying/Selling Your Home	K111		$21.95
Employment Law	K112		$21.95
Collecting Child Support	K115		$21.95
Limited Liability Company	K116		$21.95
Made E✦Z Software			
Accounting Made E-Z	SW1207		$29.95
Asset Protection Made E-Z	SW1157		$29.95
Bankruptcy Made E-Z	SW1154		$29.95
Best Career Oppportunities Made E-Z	SW1216		$29.95
Brain-Buster Crossword Puzzles	SW1223		$29.95
Brain-Buster Jigsaw Puzzles	SW1222		$29.95
Business Startups Made E-Z	SW1192		$29.95
Buying/Selling Your Home Made E-Z	SW1213		$29.95
Car Buying Made E-Z	SW1146		$29.95
Corporate Record Keeping Made E-Z	SW1159		$29.95
Credit Repair Made E-Z	SW1153		$29.95
Divorce Law Made E-Z	SW1182		$29.95
Everyday Law Made E-Z	SW1185		$29.95
Everyday Legal Forms & Agreements	SW1186		$29.95
Incorporation Made E-Z	SW1176		$29.95
Last Wills Made E-Z	SW1177		$29.95
Living Trusts Made E-Z	SW1178		$29.95
Offshore Investing Made E-Z	SW1218		$29.95
Owning a Franchise Made E-Z	SW1202		$29.95
Touring Florence, Italy Made E-Z	SW1220		$29.95
Touring London, England Made E-Z	SW1221		$29.95
Vital Record Keeping Made E-Z	SW1160		$29.95
Website Marketing Made E-Z	SW1203		$29.95
Your Profitable Home Business	SW1204		$29.95
Made E✦Z Guides			
Bankruptcy Made E-Z	G200		$17.95
Incorporation Made E-Z	G201		$17.95
Divorce Law Made E-Z	G202		$17.95
Credit Repair Made E-Z	G203		$17.95
Living Trusts Made E-Z	G205		$17.95
Living Wills Made E-Z	G206		$17.95
Last Wills Made E-Z	G207		$17.95
Small Claims Court Made E-Z	G209		$17.95
Traffic Court Made E-Z	G210		$17.95
Buying/Selling Your Home Made E-Z	G211		$17.95
Employment Law Made E-Z	G212		$17.95
Collecting Child Support Made E-Z	G215		$17.95
Limited Liability Companies Made E-Z	G216		$17.95
Partnerships Made E-Z	G218		$17.95
Solving IRS Problems Made E-Z	G219		$17.95
Asset Protection Secrets Made E-Z	G220		$17.95
Immigration Made E-Z	G223		$17.95
Buying/Selling a Business Made E-Z	G223		$17.95
Made E✦Z Books			
Managing Employees Made E-Z	BK308		$29.95
Corporate Record Keeping Made E-Z	BK310		$29.95
Vital Record Keeping Made E-Z	BK312		$29.95
Business Forms Made E-Z	BK313		$29.95
Collecting Unpaid Bills Made E-Z	BK309		$29.95
Everyday Law Made E-Z	BK311		$29.95
Everyday Legal Forms & Agreements	BK307		$29.95
Labor Posters			
Federal Labor Law Poster	LP001		$11.99
State Labor Law Poster (specify state)			$29.95
Shipping & Handling*			$
TOTAL OF ORDER:**			$

ss 1999.r2

See an item in this book you would like to order?

To order :

1. Photocopy this order form.
2. Use the photocopy to complete your order and mail to:

MADE E-Z PRODUCTS

384 S Military Trail, Deerfield Beach, FL 33442
phone: (954) 480-8933 • fax: (954) 480-8906
web site: http://www.e-zlegal.com/

‡Prices current as of 10/99

Shipping and Handling: **Add $3.50 for the first item, $1.50 for each additional item.**

****Florida residents add 6% sales tax.**

Total payment must accompany all orders.
Make checks payable to: Made E-Z Products, Inc.

Name ______________________

Company ______________________

Organization ______________________

____

Address ______________________

City ______________ State __________ Zip __________

Phone ( ) ______________________

PAYMENT:

❑ **CHECK ENCLOSED, PAYABLE TO MADE E-Z PRODUCTS, INC.**

❑ **PLEASE CHARGE MY ACCOUNT:** ❑ MasterCard ❑ VISA EXP. DATE

ACCOUNT NO.

Signature: ______________________
(required for credit card purchases)

-OR-

For faster service, order by phone:
(954) 480-8933

Or you can fax your order to us:
(954) 480-8906

Index

A-C♦♦♦♦♦

D-G♦♦♦♦♦

H-R

S-W